Terry Bradshaw

About the Book

Called the "Blond Bomber" and a "Joe Namath with knees," Terry Bradshaw was the No. 1 draft choice of the National Football League after starring as quarterback at Louisiana Tech. However, after his draft to the Pittsburgh Steelers, a team which had not earned a divisional title in 37 years, Bradshaw's career was beset with difficulties. In this exciting biography noted sportswriter Jim Benagh tells how Bradshaw overcame his problems with the press, the fans and his own game to lead the lowly Steelers to the top of pro football—winners of the Super Bowl for two consecutive years. Here is a moving story of hard-won success that every football fan will enjoy.

Terry Bradshaw
SUPERARM of PRO FOOTBALL

by Jim Benagh

G. P. PUTNAM'S SONS  NEW YORK

To Sandy

SBN: GB-399-20478-4
SBN: TR-399-60965-2
Library of Congress Cataloging in Publication Data
  Benagh, Jim
Terry Bradshaw, superarm of pro football
  (Putnam sports shelf)
  Includes index.
1. Bradshaw, Terry—Juvenile literature, 2. Football—
juvenile literature. [1. Bradshaw, Terry.
2. Football-Biography] I. Title.
GV939.B68B46 1976   796.33′2′0924 [B] [92] 75-43585
PRINTED IN THE UNITED STATES OF AMERICA
10 up

Contents

1   A Different Kind of Courage   **7**

2   "Your Time Will Come"   **12**

3   Small-College Quarterback   **23**

4   The No. 1 Choice   **38**

5   Welcome to Pittsburgh   **50**

6   Making the Team   **59**

7   Remaking the Quarterback   **70**

8   Championship Bound   **79**

9   Losing the Job   **91**

10   Who's at Quarterback?   **99**

11   Killing the "Dummy" Image   **110**

12   Life with a Winner   **121**

Index   **127**

Acknowledgements

I would like to express my appreciation to several people who were instrumental in helping me produce this book. They include John Devaney, who suggested the publisher; Charles Mercer, my editor at Putnam's; the public relations staff of the National Football League for its usual and generous help, and especially to Connie Sisler of that staff; the Pittsburgh Steelers and their publicity specialists, Ed Kiely and Joe Gordon; Mr. and Mrs. Bill Bradshaw; Lee Hedges; and O. K. (Buddy) Davis, a newspaperman from Ruston, Louisiana (*Daily Leader*), who knew all about Terry Bradshaw before any of us.

The Author

Jim Benagh is the author of numerous books and articles in the field of sports. His biography of Terry Bradshaw is the first book he has published with Putnam's. A free-lance writer, Benagh works out of Englewood Cliffs, New Jersey.

1 A Different Kind of Courage

The scene was perfect as the Pittsburgh Steelers marched their prize draft choice, quarterback Terry Bradshaw, out to the midfield of Three Rivers Stadium in April 1970, to sign him to a professional contract. At that time the stadium was still in the building stages. Workmen were installing lights almost 200 feet overhead, and the field where the Steelers would play on artificial turf in the future was still a sea of spring mud. There was much work to do.

Terry Bradshaw, like the lavishly planned stadium, was a major part of the Steelers' building plans. Thus, general manager Dan Rooney thought it would be good publicity to stage Terry's signing on the 50-yard line no matter what shape the field was in. Rooney set up a table and chairs for himself, Bradshaw, Terry's father Bill, and his attorney Robert Pugh. Photographers and television cameramen filmed the goings-on as Rooney hoped they would. The limited number of spectators, ranging from the Steelers' young coach Chuck Noll to the assortment of construction men, cheered the unique ceremony.

If everyone was so happy in Pittsburgh that Saturday afternoon, it was because the signing of Terry Bradshaw was supposed to signify the dawn of a new era in Steeler football. Here was a tremendous quarterback prospect, despite his small-college background, who was expected to perform miracles with an ancient National Football League franchise that never did learn how to win. Never mind that the well-trampled team had won only one of 14 games the season before. Terry Bradshaw, with his superarm and his enormous potential, was supposed to change all that. Never mind that 21-year-old quarterbacks did not tear up the National Football League. Terry Bradshaw was supposed to step in right away and turn the team around.

Bradshaw, at 6′ 3″ and 215 pounds, was thought to be a giant. The Steelers had never had a truly great quarterback before, and now they had the No. 1 choice of the entire college crop on their roster. There was reason to celebrate on this late April day.

Rising from the sea of mud at midfield was a wave of optimism including everyone concerned. No one expressed it more than the proud father, Bill Bradshaw, who predicted aloud that his son would "lead the Steelers to the Super Bowl in five years." In later years the elder Bradshaw admitted, "I was blowin' some smoke when I said that."

8

But confidence is the mark of a great quarterback, so there seemed to be nothing wrong if a father who raised his son to be a winner shared some of the enthusiasm. Besides, Bill Bradshaw would say years later he had really meant his boast: "Deep down, I felt it could happen if they got the people [players] to help Terry."

Dan Rooney turned to Bill Bradshaw and kiddingly told him, "If Terry can do that in five years, we'll give you a Super Bowl ring, too."

Bill Bradshaw knew that football teams aren't allowed to pass out Super Bowl rings at random, even to the men who father the players who make the Super Bowl appearances possible. But he remembered the scene five years later as the Pittsburgh Steelers held another joyous ceremony—their victory celebration in the locker room after winning Super Bowl IX in New Orleans to climax the 1974 season. Bill Bradshaw had called his shot perfectly.

But what he didn't realize on that muddy field in 1970 was the trials that his son would go through before he earned a Super Bowl ring.

For Terry Bradshaw, the most sought-after professional quarterback prospect in years, there would be a series of ups and downs such as few young players have known.

Football is a game that demands courage, and there is not a player in the National Football League who doesn't have some. But that means physical courage—the determination to give and take the punishment that sets football off from so many other games. No

9

one ever questioned Terry Bradshaw's physical courage. As a young quarterback, he was thrown into competition from the start of his rookie year and was expected to do things veteran quarterbacks do not achieve. He never flinched.

He accepted the injuries, the benchings, the quarterback sackings, the physical beatings as part of the game. When he was healthy, he never feared onrushing enemy linemen when his offensive line broke down and let him get trapped in the backfield. He was not scared to lug the football himself and smack into some 260-pound opponent in an effort to turn a 10-yard gain into an 11- or 12-yard gain. He became one of the best running quarterbacks in pro football at a time when less brave quarterbacks would scamper for the sidelines in an effort to avoid physical contact.

But Terry's real test of courage came when he had to face foes off the field. For five years, right up till the eve of Super Bowl IX, Bradshaw had to face the mental pressures put on him by his critics—hostile home fans, sniping teammates, probing sportswriters and sportscasters.

Time and again, Terry won the No. 1 quarterbacking job with the Steelers, lost it, won it back. A very religious and honest youngster, he paid for his frank comments to newsmen. Though the Steelers improved their win-loss record in each of his first five years with the team, he was the player they blamed for the club's occasional failures. And worst of all the criticism were the stories that indicated he was "dumb." No prominent quarterback in the history of the game had ever had his intelligence questioned so publicly so often.

Even in the weeks before his Super Bowl appearance in January 1975, a female sportscaster asked him point-blank during an interview, "Terry, are you really that dumb?"

In the long run, Terry proved them wrong. The strong-armed quarterback who said as a rookie, "I'm going to take the Steelers to the Super Bowl" not only took them there but led them to victory. Lesser players would have broken under the stress.

2 "Your Time Will Come"

It was March 25, 1966, in Alexandria, Louisiana, and Terry Bradshaw was finally getting some of the sports recognition he had long deserved. That day, the strong-armed but spindly-built 17-year-old high school senior lofted a javelin 240′ 2″ at the Bolton Track & Field Relays to smash the national record by more than seven feet. A week later, he lengthened the record to 243′ 7″ before a hometown audience in Shreveport, Louisiana, where he was born and raised. In no time at all he was a celebrity.

There he was—a potential Olympian who could throw the spear thirty feet farther than any other high school athlete in America. *Track & Field News, Sports Illustrated,* the Associated Press, United Press International and others gave young Bradshaw national publicity for his feats. An international track expert from Italy contacted him for additional information. Colleges began seeking him out to offer him scholarships. All the major powers, such as Southern Cal and Tennessee, wanted him badly. He was hailed as an Olympic prospect for the U. S. team in 1968, and was a long-range hope to become only the second American to win the javelin in the history of the Modern Olympics.

A high school senior could not have asked for anything more.

But Terry did.

Bradshaw was more interested in launching a professional football career than javelins. Within a few weeks, his high school track career would come to an end and he would never compete in the javelin again. Javelin throwing was only a diversion for him, a chance to test his superarm in another sport and a way of keeping his father, Bill Bradshaw, happy. It wasn't that Bill Bradshaw was pushing his sports-minded son into contests he did not want to compete in. The father merely wanted Terry to have a springtime sport to keep him occupied and away from trouble. Terry responded to his father's wishes with a series of throws in the spring of 1966 such as no other high school athlete had ever come close to matching.

Bill Bradshaw, a welder with a manufacturing firm, wanted his sons, Gary and Terry (and later, Craig), to become the athlete he never was. Bill had played some high school football in Sparta, Tennessee, and liked other sports. When Gary was born in 1947, and later Terry arrived on September 12, 1948, he could not wait to expose them to athletic contests.

At age five, Terry was already displaying the strong right arm that would later make him famous. With Gary as his catcher, Terry would pitch baseballs from 40 feet and hit the target for hours on end. His father, who was content to guide without pushing him into sports, loaned as much support as he could to the budding young star. He made Terry the batboy on the softball team he coached when Terry was only seven. At one of those games, Terry caught a stray hit ball in his chest. It was a screaming foul that permanently deformed his chest, but Terry refused to shy away from sports. At another point in his youth, Terry suffered from a cancerous growth on his left shoulder that was so serious his parents feared for his life after an operation. Still, he continued to star at baseball and once went through an entire season unbeaten as a Little League pitcher—14 victories, no defeats. He was on the mound when his Little League team upset the older Pony League players. In another season, after he began concentrating on football, he pitched three shutouts, including a perfct game, against high-class competition in Shreveport's sandlot leagues.

But football was Terry's sport from the second grade on.

Growing up in football-mad Louisiana, Terry was issued a uniform and assigned to a Pop Warner League at an age when many American boys don't even know what a football is. He fell in love with the game despite the bumps and bruises he took. When the family temporarily moved to Camanche, Iowa, for three years, Terry's football career was stifled. Camanche was not that much of a football town, and besides, young Terry was recuperating from his shoulder operation. He was forced to confine his football interest to cheering for his idol, quarterback Bart Starr of the Green Bay Packers.

There wasn't a happier kid in the world than Terry the day his family moved back to football-minded Shreveport, a city in northwestern Louisiana near the Mississippi River. Terry got himself outfitted with special shoulder pads to protect his vulnerable shoulder and went out to meet his fellow seventh-graders "jawbone to jawbone."

Unfortunately, when the junior high coach picked his team, he overlooked the smaller seventh-graders in favor of the heftier, taller eighth- and ninth-graders. Here was Terry, his heart set on professional football, and he couldn't even make a junior high team. He returned home that night a sad sight.

But Bill Bradshaw and his wife, Novice, consoled him and tried to keep his morale high.

"Your time will come," the father would say. "Just make sure that you are ready when it does."

The coach who refused to offer Terry a uniform did say that he could come to the practices. Terry did, and he eventually learned more about the game, added some size and made the team. By the time he got out of the ninth grade, he was a fine high school football prospect.

Terry was assigned to Woodlawn High School in Shreveport in 1963. He made the junior varsity as a tenth-grader. In fact, he made it with ease. But trying to get playing time on the varsity at Woodlawn High was something else. Woodlawn was a fairly new school, having been established in 1960. But by 1963, when Terry joined the Scarlet and Royal Blue Knights, the team was already a powerhouse. A veteran coach by the name of Lee Hedges had built it into a contender for the state playoffs in just a brief time after a disastrous 0-9 debut in 1960.

His teams were talented and deep. Terry made the varsity squad as a junior, but he had to sit the bench almost all season long. His rival at quarterback was Tray Prather, who would become a high school All-America in 1964. He had to watch Prather guide the team into the state playoffs instead of earning valuable experience for himself.

"It seemed that there was always a good player ahead of him," recalled Mrs. Bradshaw. "Terry got to keep the bench warm for a long time. But he was determined. He loves to compete."

Terry never got to start a varsity game before his senior year. Despite the problems, he plugged away— practicing, practicing, practicing. The Bradshaw family always knew where to find their second son. If he wasn't at Woodlawn High working out on the field or in the gymnasium working weights to build his string-bean (6′ 3″, 170-pound) body into varsity caliber, he was in the backyard of their house on Shady Lane Drive passing footballs.

Often Terry practiced alone on the family's one-acre lot. But he also worked out with a fellow classmate whom he had befriended in junior high when both were trying to become quarterback candidates. The friend was Tommy Spinks, the son of a Methodist minister. When Spinks finally realized that Terry was the better quarterback prospect, he shifted to a receiver and became Terry's favorite target. For hours at a time, Bradshaw and Spinks would drill together, waiting for the day when they would be called upon. As Bill Bradshaw had told his son, "Make sure you are ready when your time comes."

The time came in 1965 when Bradshaw and Spinks were seniors. The great 1964 Woodlawn team had been ripped by graduation losses, and a fearful season seemed to lie ahead for Hedges, who had been winning almost 75 percent of his games after that terrible first season. Bradshaw and Spinks had not even played much, and neither had most of the other nine seniors trying to salvage what seemed to be a sure losing season.

But Hedges and his backfield coach, A. L. Williams, had been keeping an eye on their junior prospects, even if they had not been playing them that much. Now that they were seniors, they would have a chance to prove themselves. In fact, they would have to prove themselves if the Knights were to continue their winning ways. Bradshaw was selected quarterback right from the start of that senior year. Spinks, who had shown so much promise, was put at wide receiver. Hedges had enough faith in this tandem to change his Winged-T offense somewhat by splitting Spinks further away from the rest of the offense when Woodlawn High lined up.

The 32-year-old coach, a former all-round star at Louisiana State, knew what he was doing as usual. In the 1965 opener, Woodlawn High overran North Caddo, 59-0. When the Knights followed up this victory with a 28-7 win over Fair Park and a 41-14 win over Bastrop, it was obvious the team would be a contender again for a state playoff berth. Crowds of 20,000 to 25,000 fans began pouring into key games in the city stadium at the Fairgrounds in Shreveport to watch Woodlawn's newest powerhouse.

The Knights got upset, 26-20, by Ouachita High in the fourth game and were being threatened by Airline High in the next contest when Bradshaw took the game into his hands. Against Airline, Terry dropped a neat screen pass into the clutches of well-placed halfback Tom Hagin, and Hagin went 65 yards with the ball. Later Bradshaw hit split receiver Spinks deep downfield with a pass that turned into a 66-yard score. Woodlawn defeated Airline, 21-20.

Woodlawn may have been looking ahead to its traditional rival Byrd High when it got tied by West Monroe, 20-20. Byrd had played the Knights every year of Woodlawn's short six-year history and always won. Each season Woodlawn would narrow the gap in the final score a bit, but even with its good teams the Knights could not handle Byrd High.

In 1965 it was a different story. Bradshaw made it so.

Guiding the team flawlessly, Terry quarterbacked the Knights to a 7-0 lead. Then he drilled a pass to Spinks that left the Byrd players befuddled. Spinks went 35 yards for a touchdown. Terry kept pouring it on, scoring once himself, until the final tally was 39-0, Woodlawn. It was a happy night for Woodlawn fans.

The Knight boosters began a countdown to another playoff berth after that game. The next two weeks would be key ones, and Woodlawn started out the stretch drive right by beating a tough Ruston High eleven, 21-14.

The following week's contest against Neville was just as rugged, and a rain-scattered field made Wood-lawn's slick attack vulnerable. In fact, with little time on the clock in the fourth quarter and Neville leading 7-6, it seemed hopeless. The only thing that had kept the Knights in the game was Terry's punts, which he was booming for a 40.3-yard average.

But with time running out, Terry made a desperation pass to Spinks. It was a last effort for the Knights, who had started deep in their own territory and hadn't yet reached midfield. Spinks caught and carried the ball far enough to get Woodlawn in field-goal range. The Knight kicker sent a beauty through the uprights with just 17 seconds left, and Woodlawn had a 9-7 victory

That clinched a playoff berth, even though there were two games left, both of which Woodlawn won with ease.

The Knights disposed of Terrebonne High, its first playoff foe, by a 13-2 score. That set up a game with powerful Lafayette High, a team that was supposed to be a shoo-in for the state championship.

Lafayette was big and powerful. Unbeaten in 12 straight games, the southern Louisiana gridders boasted a defense that did not allow any team to score more than a touchdown in any game. Furthermore, Lafayette had the benefit of playing at home.

They were supposed to be so good, Bill Bradshaw recalled, that "they wrote us off." A friend from Lafayette told the Bradshaws not to waste their time making the long trip.

But the Bradshaws did, and so did many other Shreveport fans who helped pack Lafayette's stadium. When Hedges looked up in the stands, he counted more Woodlawn fans than Lafayette fans. But the most important person in attendance proved to be Terry, whose vantage point was on the field.

In the first quarter, Terry lofted a 59-yard touchdown pass to halfback Tom Hagin. Then, picking apart the Lafayette defense with precision, Terry found a weakness and sent Hagin off on a 65-yard touchdown run. Terry passed 30 yards to his other halfback for another score. As Woodlawn began stunning the Lafayette team, Terry let loose with one pass that put fear in Lafayette players' eyes. He threw a pass so far, jaws dropped. Even Coach Hedges was in a state of shock.

Terry's intended pass traveled 65 yards through the air. It might have been caught for a touchdown, but it went so far and dropped so fast out of the air that the Woodlawn receiver could not handle it. Even the pros don't get 65 yards on their throws. But a mere 17-year-old high school kid did that night.

Bradshaw got one of his other throws closer to earth and Spinks caught it for a 40-yard play that ended near the Lafayette goal line. Terry carried the ball in on the next play and insured Woodlawn's stunning 28-13 upset.

The season ended on a sad note, however, as Woodlawn went down to defeat in the championship game. Terry got the Knights on the scoreboard with a touchdown pass to Spinks, but the rains came down and washed out Woodlawn's game plan to throw the ball. Terry ran well, but Woodlawn's lead faltered and Sulphur High School came from behind to win, 12-9.

The coach and Woodlawn fans could not be disappointed, though. The unknown quarterback had turned around what was supposed to be a mediocre season. His passing and his leadership had done a remarkable job.

Unfortunately for Terry, his skills were not that well recognized. His pet receiver Spinks, who caught over 50 of his passes, was named to the all-state team. Terry was not even all-district; he was accorded second-team all-star honors.

There were reasons why his talents did not emerge fully, however. For one thing, Woodlawn did not pass that much—only about 15 times a game. And the Winged-T offense was not geared to Bradshaw's hidden ability to carry the ball, except down near the goal line on quarterback sneaks. Terry did pass for over 1,400 yards and 21 touchdowns, but then again those are not overwhelming statistics for a 14-game season.

. Indeed, it wasn't until the Lafayette game that many colleges expressed an interest in the Woodlawn quarterback. As it turned out, most of the big recruiting

rush would come after his Herculean javelin throws—
and the athletic scholarship offers would be for track,
not football.

Terry did get a football offer from Louisiana State,
and he came close to taking it. But Tray Prather was
there, and Terry did not want to sit the bench again,
waiting for his old teammate to graduate. Báylor University, a Baptist-affiliated school in Texas, wooed
Terry, too, but few other big-time schools expressed
an interest.

When Terry finally sifted through his handful of
offers, he chose a small college not too far from Shreveport. The school was Louisiana Tech, in Ruston.

His choice was based on several considerations. He
felt he would have a better chance to play sooner. And
he felt, with only one full season of solid football behind him, that would be important if he was ever going
to play professional football. He had friends there, and
teammate Spinks would go along with him.

But Tech was a virtual unknown to big-time football fans. And it seemed to most observers that the
strong-armed javelin thrower would wind up just a
passing fancy who had once led a high school team to
a runner-up spot in Louisiana high school football.
There were track coaches, but few football coaches,
who wanted to cry over the thought.

3 Small-College Quarterback

Louisiana Tech was a good-sized school with about 7,000 students when Terry Bradshaw arrived there in the heat of August 1966. But despite the enrollment, Tech was considered in the small-college ranks and therefore freshmen could play for the varsity.* Thus the quarterback prospect, along with his high school buddy and favorite receiver Tommy Spinks, were assembled with the rest of the returning Bulldog squad for team and individual photographs.

Terry was as raw as the next freshman. Maybe even rawer. Quarterbacks are supposed to look and act like leaders as well as be leaders. The gawky, slowpoke appearance of the 17-year-old yearling from Shreveport just didn't seem to fit the mold.

---

* In 1972 the National Collegiate Athletic Association passed a rule making freshman eligible to play for any team, big-time or small-college.

As the team members idled around and waited for the photos to be taken, some veterans started making fun of the "hayseed blond" with the deep country accent. Local newspaperman O. K. (Buddy) Davis of the Ruston *Daily Leader* was one of those who heard the harmless prodding that so many freshmen must go through. When the teasing got to be too much, Bradshaw abruptly turned to the veterans and announced bluntly: "That's okay. I'm going to be the first No. 1 draft choice this school has ever had."

The older players, and newspaperman Davis, too, couldn't help but laugh.

But freshman Bradshaw was already planning his future—and working hard at it. In the summer of 1966, he arrived early at the Tech campus in Ruston, a town of about 18,000 people in north-central Louisiana, and began searching for somebody to work out with. He and friend Spinks found some willing high school stars in local heroes Bert Jones and Andy Hamilton.

Jones, a quarterback, was the son of Dub Jones, a former star halfback with the Cleveland Browns when they were winning National Football League titles left and right in the 1950s. In fact, the senior Jones set a record by scoring six touchdowns in a single game against the Chicago Bears in 1951. That equaled the record of six set by Hall of Famer Ernie Nevers back in 1929, and it would take another Hall of Fame type player, Gale Sayers, to match it in 1965. Hamilton, a lithe receiver, was Dub Jones's nephew.

The Jones clan, with Dub directing them, and the

twosome from Shreveport couldn't get in enough football despite the blazing hot Louisiana heat.

Bert Jones, who would later star at Louisiana State and become a No. 1 draft choice in the NFL, and Bradshaw loved to throw the ball. They were forever having contests—whether it was throwing footballs, rocks or javelins. Mostly, though, they were pitching footballs to Hamilton (who also would make it to the NFL) and Spinks.

"We did go at it until we wore ourselves out," said Terry. "We did it because we liked it so much. I loved to practice. The way we looked at it was, if you're ever going to be anything, you have to sacrifice some of your lazy-hour time practicing."

The foursome, and anyone else who wanted to get into the drills, would start at about eight o'clock each morning and play right through till lunchtime. Then after a snack and a swim they would go at it again. Mostly it was Jones and Hamilton versus Bradshaw and Spinks, two-on-two games. In the evenings, Dub Jones would be home from work and lend his professional expertise to the sessions. The Joneses and the Hamiltons made it much easier for a couple of lonely freshmen away from home for the first time.

Once the school year began, Bradshaw came under the tutelage of Tech coach Joe Aillet, a veteran of some 25 years at the school. Bradshaw continued to work hard, but he could work his way up the ranks no higher than No. 2 quarterback behind sophomore Phil Robertson.

Coach Aillet liked the looks of his freshman, who

was zinging the ball with the same velocity that earned him recognition in high school—and maybe harder. In fact, the coach was quoted as saying, "Terry throws the ball harder than any freshman I've ever seen—maybe as hard as *anyone* I've ever seen."

But the coach's compliments were not converted into confidence when it came time to get into games. Robertson was the starter and monopolized the playing time. Tech was having a horrendous year—the Bulldogs won only one game—so the coach figured he'd go with his best player to save face. Once, when Robertson got hurt, Bradshaw was put in the line of fire and played a respectable game. But the next week Robertson was healthy again and earned his job back. The fact that Robertson was only a sophomore discouraged Terry, who could see himself sitting the bench for two more seasons before getting a chance to play regularly.

The Bulldogs finished with a miserable 1-9 record and sent Aillet into early retirement. When Terry found out that Max Lambright, basically a ground-oriented coach, would replace Aillet, his star dimmed even darker. Bradshaw made up his mind that he was going to transfer out of Tech and went so far as driving all the way to Tallahassee, Florida, to see if pass-minded Florida State might give him a chance. But once he got there, Florida State told him to turn around and go back to Tech, where he belonged.

Bradshaw did. The 1967 season proved to be more promising even if he couldn't dislodge Robertson from the starting role. Terry at least got in some playing time, and teaming often with high school buddy Spinks and roommate Larry Brewer, he passed for 951 yards. His strong-armed throws earned him the nickname "The Blond Bomber" from his teammates.

Lambright had more insight than Terry had given him credit for. The coach knew a diamond in the rough when he saw one. To help Terry and the other Tech quarterbacks polish their passing game, he brought in Mickey Slaughter, a former Tech quarterback and onetime Denver Bronco star, as assistant coach. In the meantime, Bradshaw's rival, Robertson, quit the team after the 1967 season and Terry was elevated to a starting role. No longer would he be discouraged in any way with the Tech situation.

Terry continued to work hard to justify his position as Tech's starting quarterback for the 1968 season. Slaughter, who was quick to realize Terry's potential, worked hard with him. Tech had won only three games in 1966, bringing its two-year record to 4-16, so there was no problem in convincing Lambright to give up his rushing offense for the more exciting pro-style passing game. The fact that Terry could lug a football as well as he could pass one helped in the decision.

The 1968 season opened at Starkville, Mississippi, where Tech was expected to be a hapless warmup foe for Mississippi State University of the powerful major-college Southeastern Conference. State was no powerhouse, coming off a 1-9 season, but Tech had no right to be confident that September 21 evening. The last time Tech played a major-college team was in the final game of the 1967 season and it lost, 58-7. For 1968 the sportswriters had picked Tech to finish dead-last in its 10-team Gulf States Conference football race.

Somehow, the Tech Bulldogs and the Mississippi State Bulldogs engaged in a dogfight for over three quarters that neither team was used to seeing in recent years. Terry survived a mediocre first half, in which he hit only 5 of 12 passes for 52 yards, and depended on his defensive teammates to hold State in check.

The score was 13-10, State leading, in the middle of the fourth quarter when Bradshaw finally rallied his forces and drove the team into field-goal range. Tech tied the game on a 33-yarder. Soon after, Tech had the ball again on its own 24-yard line. Terry began another drive, which looked like it was going to end when his team found itself in a fourth-down-and-10 situation on the State 37. There were only 2:21 minutes left in the game, but the Tech coaching staff decided to put its faith in the young quarterback and go for broke.

Bradshaw sent Tommy Spinks out on a pattern in which he curled in toward the middle of the field. Then, with the pressure on him and his receiver, Bradshaw rifled a perfect pass which Spinks grabbed and went in to score. Tech made the extra point and held on in the final minutes for a surprising 20-13 victory.

Bradshaw's passing statistics weren't that impressive— 12 for 30—but the way he handled the ball club was enough to convince the coaches that their decision to play the passing game was right.

The next week Bradshaw had to play only two quarters, completing over half of his 15 passes to lead the Bulldogs to another victory over a major-college team.

This time East Carolina was the victim, 35-7, in front of the home fans at Ruston.

The following two weeks were not good ones for Tech, as they opened Gulf States Conference play with two straight defeats. But Terry could hardly be blamed. In a 27-20 loss to McNeese State, Terry led his team back from a 17-0 deficit to take the lead, then see it dwindle away. He completed 20 of his 38 passes for 319 yards and all three Tech touchdowns.

In the McNeese game, Terry began to show the coolness under pressure that would be his trademark at Tech. After his 52-yard scoring pass was called back, he sent the same receiver out on the same pattern on the very next play—and got the TD again. Later in the game, he saw his pass for a two-point conversion nullified by a penalty, but he got the two back by throwing the same pass to the other side of the field.

In the other loss, to Southwestern Louisiana, Terry hit on 28 of 47 passes for 432 yards and all three of his team's TDs. He also ran for 38 yards. But Tech lost, 28-24.

At a time when it looked as if Tech might be the last-place team in the Conference, just as the "experts" had predicted, the Bulldogs needed a lift. Their next game would be against an old rival, Northwestern Louisiana, which had been playing Tech since 1907. The game was set for Shreveport, Terry's hometown. NW Louisiana carried a four-game winning streak into the game and rolled up a 19-7 halftime lead.

Bradshaw didn't give his hometown followers much to cheer about in that half, connecting on only 2-of-12 passes. But in the second half, he had the record crowd of 30,000 in his corner. NW Louisiana kept scoring but Bradshaw went after them, making three TDs himself on keeper plays and passing for two more as his team came within four points, 39-35, with less than three minutes to play.

Tech got the ball again and drove to their foe's 19, where the drive ended when Terry's pass was intercepted. Tech didn't get the ball again until there were only 25 seconds left. At that juncture, the Bulldogs were on their own 18-yard line. Bradshaw had little choice but to test his arm against the whole opposing team. He called for flanker Ken Liberto to run a "go" pattern— that is, just shoot downfield—and Terry would try to get the ball to him. A touchdown was necessary; a field goal wasn't enough.

Liberto lit out like his jersey was on fire. Meanwhile, Bradshaw dropped back well beyond the line of scrimmage, turned and lofted a long ball the way he used to peg javelins. He nailed Liberto on the opponents' 35-yard line, and the flanker was moving so fast he went right on to the end zone. The pass had traveled almost 60 yards through the air and ended up on target, a perfect strike. The 30,000 fans, to say nothing of the opponents, were in awe as Tech walked off the field with a next-to-impossible 42-39 triumph.

The next week, against another major-college foe, Southern Mississippi, Bradshaw did it again. With his team down, 7-0, he lofted a 70-yard scoring pass to Liberto, then drove his team to a 21-7 victory.

By now, the pro scouts were beginning to hear about

this passing and ball-handling wizard out of little Louisiana Tech. A representative of the Boston (now New England) Patriots said, "Bradshaw is by far the best pro prospect for quarterback I have seen this year. He doesn't lose his cool and he can really fire the ball." Terry's friend Dub Jones, who got to see him play almost every game, said, "Terry is the best college passer I've seen. He's just fabulous. He scrambles better than Fran Tarkenton when he has to. You won't find anybody with more credentials."

For the rest of the season, Bradshaw continued his heroics and wound up leading small-college players in total offense with 2,987 yards—almost 250 more than the runner-up. In the passing department, he connected on 176 of 339 for a 51.9 percentage rate and 22 touchdowns. He set 15 school records.

And the statistics were even more impressive when you consider that four of his ten games were against major-college foes. In the last of those games, against New Mexico State, Terry threw for 445 yards and four touchdowns and ran for 34 more yards as he took part in a record 60 plays.

Then for a topper to a magnificent season, he led Tech to a 33-13 victory over Akron University in the Grantland Rice Bowl. In that game, he ran for two TDs and passed for two more and rolled up another ton of yardage that didn't count in the annual statistics because it was a post-season game.

The game enhanced his professional potential, however, when scouts of many northern-climate teams watched him perform his magic in sub-freezing temperatures and 25-mile winds. It was the first time Terry had played under such conditions and on a snow-blown field. Many a lesser Southern-bred quarterback would have cooled his performance under such conditions.

But the people who knew the cool-under-fire quarterback over the past season did not expect him to do less than "fire under the cool" in the finale. Terry had lived up to the All-America billing he received for his 1968 performance.

The pro scouts had been trickling down to the Ruston area for years, but mostly to stay there while they scouted the players at Grambling College a few miles away. The year 1969 would be a treat for the scouts. They could visit Grambling and Tech on the same trip. And they did, beginning with Terry's spring practices.

There was a lot of pressure on the 20-year-old "Blond Bomber" that spring. He couldn't pick up a football without attracting a crowd of some of the elite of pro football scouting. When Tech finally wound up its spring drills with its intrasquad game, nearly the whole New Orleans Saints staff, including head coach Tom Fears, was on hand. The Saints were a losing team in the 1968 standings, and there was a good possibility they would have a chance to get Terry if they finished in last place in 1969. Terry liked that possibility, too.

"It would be nice to stay in Louisiana and play for New Orleans," he told eager reporters from the state's newspapers. But the pressures he put on himself by thinking about the Saints staff in the stands caused him to play a mediocre spring game. He vowed that when the senior season came, he wouldn't make the same mistake again. "I blew my cool," he admitted. "But I learned my lesson. Now I will play even that much harder."

After working out under the hot Louisiana sun all summer, Terry set a goal to lead the Bulldogs to an unbeaten season in 1969. The team would be a good one, and Terry's receivers had become well accustomed to his bulletlike passes. He was a little concerned personally because some critics suggested that he might fold under the pressure of being so highly touted. He set a goal of 3,000 passing yards to prove them wrong.

The goal for an unbeaten season ended with a midyear 24-23 loss to Southern Mississippi. And his goal of 3,000 passing yards fell short by almost 700 yards. But the reason for the latter failure was because Terry was too good for his own good, and Tech was a much better team.

Week after week, Tech rolled up huge scores on the opposition—24, 35, 34, 42, 55, 23, 25, 77 and 34 points in regular-season games. More often than not, those high scores were registered early in the games and the first string was pulled to save the opposition from embarrassment. Even in the only defeat, Terry passed 46 times for 21 completions, 278 yards and two touchdowns.

After the season was five games old, he had played only two series of downs in the five fourth quarters combined.

But he showed the pro scouts what they had come to see, even if it was abbreviated. In a midyear game against Chattanooga, with six scouts in the stands,

Terry threw an early 20-yard TD pass. Then there was a power failure and the lights were out for an hour and a half as the scouts cringed and twisted in their seats. The game was only five minutes old and some of them were viewing—or trying to view—Terry for the first time.

When the lights came on again, Bradshaw lit up the sky with passes. On the first play, he passed for 38 yards. Then he drove his team into the end zone, carrying the ball across himself for the final yard. Before the first period was over, he had 8-for-9 in the passing department (for 133 yards and two TDs) and his team was ahead 28-0. He was pulled for the second quarter, but in the third period Coach Lambright decided to send the regulars back in so they would not get rusty. All Terry did was throw a 76-yard scoring pass on the first play, which cost him a chance to throw again that night.

But the pro scouts got an eyeful while they watched.

"He's a big Sammy Baugh," gulped Jim Lee Howell, a scout for the New York Giants and a player and coach in the Baugh era.

Terry by now had blossomed to about 215 pounds on his six-foot three-inch frame, and his running speed of 4.6 seconds for the 40-yard dash was more than the pros required from quarterbacks. His courage in banging through the line showed the pros he was more than merely a drop-back passer. "He is," said one scout, "a Joe Namath with knees."

Tech lost only one game in the regular season as

Terry increased his school records to 22—the most possible for a quarterback. He again was the All-America quarterback and was fast becoming the darling of fans nationally as well as sportswriters and the pro scouts. Little Ruston had become more than a stopping-off point on the way to Grambling College.

"Terry Bradshaw probably brought more recognition to Tech and Ruston in the past two years than any other individual in the school's and city's history," said sportswriter Davis of the *Daily Leader* at a banquet.

There would be more publicity to come—his picture on the covers of *Sports Illustrated, Newsweek* and *The Sporting News.*

The quarterback had closed out his regular-season play with some highly impressive statistics, even if they didn't match those of his junior year. He was third in the nation in total offense with 2,484 yards (the two players who finished slightly above him each played one more game). His passing accuracy improved to 54.8 percent (248 attempts, 136 completions), even if his total yardage and touchdowns took a dip.

That gave Terry a four-year total of 6,589 yards rushing and passing. No other Louisiana college player had ever surpassed 5,000. Considering that Terry was only a starter for two years, that total is even more remarkable.

There was a disappointing bowl game loss, 34-14, to East Tennessee State in his final outing in a Tech jersey, but Bradshaw more than made up for that setback in two post-season all-star games.

In the first of those games, the North-South contest in Miami, Florida, Terry got a little taste of what it would be like to play with a team full of stars. In a practice session he took the snap from center and spun around to hand off to lightning starter Norm Bulaich, a halfback from Texas Christian. Terry thrust the ball out, but only to find that Bulaich had already dashed through the hole. He stood there almost red faced, wondering what the coaches were thinking about this hayseed quarterback from the small college playing with all these blue-chippers from big schools. But Bradshaw got into the North-South game and fared well.

In a more important contest, the Senior Bowl All-Star Game in Mobile, Alabama, Terry was magnificent. The Senior Bowl gives a player such as Terry, from a small school, a chance to show the pros what he can do in topflight competition. The January 1970 Senior Bowl included many of the players who had starred for their regular teams in bowl games and now would be making their final appearances before the draft. Almost every head coach in the National Football League attended the game, too, so that they could double-check the scouting reports they had been receiving on players throughout the year.

Terry, playing for the South team, lived up to all the scouting reports on him—and then some. In a wide-open 37-37 tie game, he passed for 267 yards and two touchdowns, driving his team up and down field all day long. He completed 17 of his 31 attempts. He was clearly the Most Valuable Player of the game and he left the pro coaches in the stands drooling.

The Pittsburgh Steelers and the Chicago Bears, who shared last place in the NFL standings, could not wait to make the coin flip that would decide who would have the first opportunity to draft this small-college phenom.

4 The No. 1 Choice

The National Football League's annual draft of college players is like a winter ritual. The pro teams are given an order in which the players will be taken, based upon their own standings during the previous season. The lowest teams draft ahead of the better teams in an effort to balance the league.

However, a team is allowed to trade its draft choice for existing star pro players if it feels that will be more beneficial. Football fans, too, like to follow this "game within a game" as they make up mythical trades for their teams or have side bets as to who will be taken by whom. The newspapermen and television announcers, hungry for some good off-season football news, carefully cover the draft with major stories before and after the late January proceedings. For everyone involved, including the draftees, it's a guessing game with intrigue.

The intrigue as to who would be made the very first choice in the 1970 draft was mellowed somewhat because Terry Bradshaw's name was the first mentioned in almost all the pro scouts' conversations. His great junior season in 1968 at Louisiana Tech had brought him to the attention of the pros, and he did not do anything in the 1969 season to lower his superb rating.

The fact that he starred in the North-South Game and, more important, in the Senior Bowl All-Star Game, underscored his value to the pro scouts. One of the pro representatives at the Senior Bowl was none other than Pittsburgh Steelers head coach Chuck Noll. He was most impressed. "Terry was handicapped by a pulled hamstring muscle and a rib injury but went through those two all-star games without flinching," said Noll. "You have to get closeups to judge accurately. Terry convinced me that he was the most valuable piece of property in the college ranks. He is an extremely accurate drop-back passer and he can take off and run with the ball if necessary."

Over the past year, other pros had been openly high on the rifle-armed quarterback from Tech, too. Don Klosterman, the general manager of the Houston Oilers and a former star quarterback himself, told a reporter that Bradshaw might be the best quarterback prospect *ever* to come out of college ball. Gil Brandt, the astute general manager of the Dallas Cowboys and the man in charge of pro football's best scouting network, had predicted before the start of Terry's senior year that he would probably be the first player taken.

"He can really throw," said Brandt. "He's got a real quick delivery and he's accurate. I'd liken his quickness of delivery to Joe Namath's." Ray Renfro, the Dallas assistant coach in charge of receivers, also watched Bradshaw. "He's the best I've seen this year. He's got such an arm that he doesn't have to be in balance when he's throwing the ball. It makes me sick that we won't have a chance to draft him." (Dallas for several years had been one of the best teams in football and thus one of the last teams to draft on the first round.)

There were other pro-Bradshaw comments, saying almost the exact things Noll, Klosterman, Brandt and Renfro had said. But it was Noll's word that counted the most.

During the 1969 season, Noll's Pittsburgh team had finished dead-last in the National Football League's Century Division with a 1-13 record. The Chicago Bears likewise had a 1-13 record, so a coin flip was arranged during Super Bowl week to decide which team—the Steelers or the Bears—would get the very first draft pick. Pittsburgh won the flip and from then on had the luxury of deciding which player in all of college football it wanted to draft on the first round.

Once Noll saw Terry at the Senior Bowl practices and game, his mind was made up. What he saw reinforced what the Steelers scouts had been saying all year long.

Noll's Steelers could have used any of a number of college stars. His 1969 team (it was his first season as head coach) suffered in many departments besides quarterback. The defense gave up 404 points—the worst in pro football that season. Mike McKoy, a superstrong tackle at Notre Dame, would have made a good No. 1 choice to go along with Pittsburgh's outstanding rookie, Joe Greene, to patch up the defensive line. The Steelers needed receivers and defensive backs, too.

The team could have gotten more than one star through the trading of the No. 1 draft choice. The offers began pouring in right after the Steelers won the coin flip. Almost every team dangled an offer in front of the Steelers' vice president Dan Rooney in an effort to be in position to draft Bradshaw. The Steelers figured it did not cost them anything to hear everyone out. According to Rooney, about four of the offers were very tempting.

The St. Louis Cardinals were willing to give up their own No. 1 choice, which would be further down the list, plus five potential starting players. The Philadelphia Eagles put together a list of four players they said would be possible starters for Pittsburgh. So did the Oakland Raiders. The Atlanta Falcons supposedly opened their bidding with a comment by Coach Norm Van Brocklin, a former All-Pro quarterback, who said, "Take what you want and take as many as you want." A total of 17 teams made a pitch of some sort.

But what Pittsburgh would finally end up asking for would be too much for other teams to come up with. "Most of these offers never got beyond the inquiry stage," said Dan Rooney. "We weren't interested in what they were offering and they weren't interested in what we wanted."

What Pittsburgh wanted, management said, was a "Superman." If it could not get one in a trade for the No. 1 draft choice, it would settle for "Superarm" himself.

Because Bradshaw's reputation had ballooned by draft day, January 27, many of the Pittsburgh fans let it be known they would settle for "Superarm." The Steelers had had the very first pick in the draft twice in the past 35 years. Many fans fondly remembered the choice of big Bill Dudley, an exciting running back, in 1942; he became one of the best and most popular players in Steelers history. The other No. 1 pick was Gary Glick, a surprise choice who had only moderate success in the pros.

There were some doubts among the experts, however, right down to the opening of the draft at the Roosevelt Hotel in New York City that the Steelers would keep the No. 1 pick and go with Bradshaw. The reasoning behind the doubts was twofold. For one thing, no National Football League team in the first 34 years of the draft had ever selected a small-college player as the first player picked. (However, the Kansas City Chiefs of the American League had taken monstrous tackle Buck Buchanan of Grambling College, the all-black school just 15 miles east of Ruston, Louisiana, as the first player in 1963, and he became an All-Pro star.)

Furthermore, the history of the National Football League draft proved that quarterbacks taken as the very first picks did not fare very well. A total of 10 had been selected in the first 34 years. Only one of them,

Heisman Trophy winner Paul Hornung of Notre Dame, became a real star—and he was shifted from quarterback to running back by Coach Vince Lombardi after he was chosen by the Green Bay Packers. The other nine quarterbacks included very few men who even earned starting jobs in the pros and a few outright "busts."

Another problem with choosing a quarterback is that it takes time for him to develop—usually three or four years for the best prospects. Even for a Terry Bradshaw, who had quarterbacked from a pro-type offense throughout most of his high school and college career, there would be many things to learn and adjustments to be made. Some critics felt that the Steelers, who needed immediate help in so many departments, would have been better off making the trade.

When the morning of January 27, 1970, rolled around, Bradshaw got up early. It would be a big day in his life no matter who took him in the draft because he had heard all the rumors and knew how highly the pros rated him. He decided to return home to Shreveport for the draft, but he wasn't at his house the night before when the Chicago Bears tried to reach him. The fact that they called (the Bears had the second pick in the draft) made him think that they were the team that would take him.

At 9 A.M. on the morning of the 27th, Bradshaw sat down near the telephone and prepared for the final answer.

Nine o'clock Shreveport time is 8 A.M., New York time, and for some reason Terry thought the draft began then. Actually it began an hour later, so Terry began getting nervous. "I thought they had forgotten me," he said later. He had figured all along that the Steelers would trade either Terry Hanratty, the rookie who quarterbacked the team the year before, or himself. When no announcement to either effect was made, Bradshaw was left in a state of confusion. Then his miscalculation of the starting time of the draft added to his bewilderment.

But 15 minutes before the draft commenced, Steelers owner Art Rooney, Sr., a kind old man who had purchased the team back in the early 1930s and suffered through almost four decades without a champion, made a phone call to the Bradshaw home in Shreveport to inform him that the Steelers were going to make him the No. 1 choice. It was a dream come true for Terry. "I was honored that they thought so much of me," he said. "I was thrilled to death. It was great, man, the greatest day of my life."

A little while later, the draft began. Each team made its choices from its own office and they were called into New York, where National Football League Commissioner Pete Rozelle made the announcement in a big ballroom in the Roosevelt Hotel.

Though Bradshaw already knew his status, there was yet one more stage of confusion before his name was announced. As fans buzzed among themselves in a special gallery set up for them in the ballroom, the Steelers used up exactly five minutes and 50 seconds of their allotted six minutes before Rozelle went to the microphone and said, "The Pittsburgh Steelers open the 1970 draft by taking quarterback Terry Bradshaw of Louisiana Tech." The buzzing in the crowd and among newsmen stopped, and everybody nodded their heads as if they had known all along.

The reason for the delay, apparently, was that the trade winds were blowing right up to the deadline and Bradshaw was the name being blown around the most. The St. Louis Cardinals especially were trying to make a deal going down to the wire. And there was that thought in the back of Dan Rooney's head, right to the finish, that "Somebody could offer us Superman."

For the rest of the morning, Terry still had to live with the fact that he might be traded. As newsmen called him for quotes, he kept asking the same question back: "I've heard all morning that they're going to trade me; have you heard that?"

The newsmen kept telling him no, they had not heard a thing. And each time, Terry's happiness was re-inforced.

"I sure hope they don't get rid of me," he'd say.

Among the questions most asked was the one about money. How much would Terry command now that he was officially the top pick among all the available collegians.

"I haven't the slightest idea," he'd tell them. And he was honest about his answer.

Before the draft even neared, Terry had made a trip around the country—to all-star games, award dinners, etc. Whenever he could, he spoke to star pros about the money angle and how he should pursue it. Should he enlist an agent to deal for him? And if not, what should he do? And how much should he ask?

In Los Angeles, star quarterback Roman Gabriel told Terry to forget about the agents. All they would do was take 10 percent, or so, of his money and not do that much for him. He would be better off, Gabriel said, getting a good lawyer he trusted and let that lawyer write a solid contract for a fee.

Other players in other towns told him the same thing. So Terry lined up a respected Shreveport lawyer, Robert Pugh, to do his bargaining. Pugh was a prominent adviser in labor negotiations so he could be tough in contract talks. He could handle all the legal matters that were above the 21-year-old college senior's head and get him as good a contract as an agent could. Besides, Terry wanted to get his contract written and over with. He wasn't out to make a killing by stalling tactics, and he said so in public.

"I'm not going to play it like those guys [he mentioned a couple of high 1969 draft choices] did last year," he said. "Football means too much to me. I'll try to get all I can. But I'll be to camp on time." The players he was talking about had held out so long they missed part of their training camps in August.

Several agents had been trying to woo Bradshaw for weeks before the draft and some came on strong after he was made the No. 1 pick. But Terry had made up his mind that Pugh would handle the negotiations and "keep all the dogs off my back."

As it turned out, Terry and the Steelers didn't even talk about money for a week after the draft. He figured he'd get a six-figure ($100,000 or more) contract. But his needs were not that greeedy and in later years he once told Steelers owner Art Rooney, Sr., he would have signed for $15,000 if that's all the pros were paying their players.

The rest of the day of January 27 was spent hearing the results of the draft and wondering how his new team, the Steelers, were faring in their second, third, fourth and other lower-round picks. As Terry would learn later, the Steelers did quite well.

On the second round, Pittsburgh selected Ron Shanklin, a North Texas State player who also starred in the Senior Bowl. A 6′ 1″ 190-pounder with blazing speed, Shanklin had caught 56 passes for 874 yards and 10 touchdowns his senior year. He would be a great wide receiver for the Steelers, who were surprised that he was still around in the second phase of the draft.

Tht Steelers got another player who would help them in the third round when they selected a swift defensive back, Mel Blount of Southern University, in Baton Rouge, Louisiana. And in the fifth round, they picked up another fine receiver named Jon Staggers, from the University of Missouri. He also was a fine kick returner. And they got yet another fine receiver on the eighth round in Dave Smith of Indiana (Pennsylvania) State College.

Then, to top off a fine day, came the announcement

from Dan Rooney that "we did not come close to making a trade."

"The basis of our decision to draft Bradshaw," he continued, "is to strive to produce a championship team as soon as possible. We are not just interested in respectability in between."

It was made clear that Terry would have to battle three other experienced quarterbacks for the job. They were Terry Hanratty, last year's rookie starter at the end of the season, and two veterans—Dick Shiner and Kent Nix—who had started National Football League games. Obviously, no pro team would keep all four. But Bradshaw was ready to meet the challenge.

"I think I have the ability to start and if I get the chance I'm sure I can produce," he told reporters on draft day. "What I want to do most is make Pittsburgh a winner. Pittsburgh has been having bad luck. But I got it set in my mind that I wanted to go up there.

"I know that I have to prove myself, that I won't be the starter just because I was their first draft pick. But I know they'll give me a chance to learn and win a job."

Whatever the case, this January day Terry Bradshaw had made history. He was the No. 1 choice in all of football, and thus the pressure would be on him to prove himself. Year after year, at draft time, writers redo their old stories about all the No. 1 picks who have failed—and how that distinction only adds to the pressures on a first-year man. They wrote of the great ones —the Heisman Trophy winners like Terry Baker, Ernie Davis, Billy Cannon, Bob Fenimore, Tom Harmon—

48

and others who didn't make it for a number of reasons. Now they were writing about a small-college star who didn't even come close in reputation with those other players.

What chance would a Terry Bradshaw have?

"Terry who? From Louisiana what?" one prominent sportswriter in Pennsylvania wrote right after the draft.

5 Welcome to Pittsburgh

When a *Sports Illustrated* reporter came down to interview Terry after the draft, the beaming blond quarterback told him outright, "All along, I wanted to go with a loser. I never wanted to go with L.A. or Minnesota or any good team. I wanted to go someplace like Chicago or Pittsburgh, where if I made it they would make it with me."

The reporter jotted down every word Terry said and a week later the magazine, with Bradshaw's picture on the cover, came out. The story was headlined: I WANTED TO GO WITH A LOSER.

Well, being picked by Pittsburgh in the draft, Terry could not have found a bigger loser in pro football history. Here was a team, started by a gentlemanly person named Art Rooney in 1933, that had gone 37 straight years without even a divisional title. In those 37 years, the team won 162 games compared to 267 losses. There had been head coaching shifts 16 different times.

The Steelers were the NFL's most notorious losers, with only eight winning (above .500) seasons in their past. They went 10 seasons after their founding before they put together their first winning team. Then the next year, 1943, their ranks were depleted so badly that they were combined with the Philadelphia Eagles franchise just so they could put a representative team on the field during the World War II year. The team was renicknamed "the Steegles," and it had a rough time winning. The next year the Steelers were merged with the Chicago Cardinals (forerunners of the St. Louis Cardinals), and those two franchises combined finished with an 0-10-0 record, the worst in Steeler history. Before Terry joined the team, the Steelers' all-time records against traditional rivals in the NFL read like this:

Vs. Philadelphia:	won 22, lost 40, tied 1
Vs. Cleveland:	won 9, lost 31
Vs. Washington:	won 28, lost 36, tied 4
Vs. Los Angeles:	won 1, lost 11, tied 2
Vs. Chicago (Bears):	won 2, lost 15, tied 1
Vs. Green Bay:	won 7, lost 18
Vs. New York (Giants):	won 24, lost 41, tied 3

Before the 1970 draft, the last time they had had a good team was in 1962, when Bobby Layne quarterbacked them to a 9-5-0 season. But even then, the Steelers were outscored during the season, 312 points to 363 for the opponents. After that, it was all downhill until 1969, when they hit rock bottom with their 1-13-0 record in Chuck Noll's first year as a head coach. In 1969, the Steelers won their first game, then dropped 13 straight. They gave up 404 points, one of the worst defensive marks in pro football history.

One problem in the history of the Steelers' franchise seemed to be its love affair with rock-'em, sock-'em type of football. The University of Pittsburgh had some of the greatest college teams in the 1930s—they were known for their shutouts. So the local pro team, trying to capture the college audience for its own gate, tried playing the same way. The Steelers seemed to think "offense" was something you did with the ball after you jarred loose a fumble or intercepted a pass. Even the nickname "Steelers" denoted a rock-ribbed defense rather than a loose, free-flowing offense. Art Rooney, Sr., once said that the rock-'em, sock-'em game was bred into the players so thoroughly that when they played the great Cleveland Browns teams of the 1950s, with their flashy passing attack led by Otto Graham, the Steeler players used to go up to the Browns after the game and tell them they ought to be playing basketball if they wanted to pass so much.

One problem with the Steelers was that they rarely had a quarterback who could help them in the speeded-up game of pro football. Probably the best in Pittsburgh history was Bobby Layne, the potbellied Texan, who didn't join the team until 1958. He had played his greatest years beforehand with the Detroit Lions, leading them to several championships. Then he only played with the Steelers through 1962, when his arm was so bad he almost had to shot-put his passes. Despite his short term with the Steelers, he set team records for most passing yardage and most touchdowns (67).

It wasn't that the Steelers didn't have an opportunity to sign a good quarterback. During their post-World War II history, when the passing game became the main threat in pro football, they had on their team such quarterbacks as Johnny Unitas, Len Dawson, Jackie Kemp, Earl Morrall and Bill Nelsen. Unfortunately, the Steelers cut or traded each one of those fine passers before they blossomed into true NFL stars. Each one of those quarterbacks led a team to a league championship *after* he left Pittsburgh, and most of them became All-League and/or Most Valuable Players with their new teams.

No wonder the Pittsburgh fans loudly voiced their opinion that the No. 1 draft choice—and a chance to select Superarm Bradshaw—should not be traded. The Steeler fans wanted to find out what it would be like to have a quarterback on their side of the scrimmage line for a change.

The acquisition of Bradshaw caused many Pittsburgh fans to make the comparison of him with Joe Namath, the strong-armed passer who was considered the best in football after leading his New York Jets team to a Super Bowl upset in 1969. The comparison was inevitable because Namath was a local boy, having grown up in Beaver Falls, Pennsylvania, just outside Pittsburgh. Like Terry, he was a glamorous personality.

But when Bradshaw kept hearing his name bracketed

with Namath's, he wanted the comparison to stop after the discussion of their passing arms.

Terry was basically a country boy, well rooted in religion and shyness.

"I'm no Joe Namath," he would tell reporters who were forever trying to find common denominators between the two. "I've been brought up differently. The long hair and the curly sideburns don't fit my 'image. I don't want to be like him. I don't know that much about him except what I hear. I'm more of a churchgoer. I owe everything I have to the Man up there and I aim to do as much good as I can to pay Him back."

Terry wasn't going out of his way to put down Namath or offend Joe's huge following in the Pittsburgh area where high school football is one of the biggest pastimes for the sons of tough old steel-mill workers, many from the same Eastern European backgrounds as Namath's parents, who were of Hungarian descent. But the sportswriters asked him questions, and he tried to be as honest as he could.

That honesty would get him in trouble from time to time.

When Terry would talk about going up to Pittsburgh and taking over as the quarterback so the team could have a winner, some fans felt that Bradshaw was belittling Terry Hanratty, a local boy who had played his high school ball in the same league as Namath's before joining the Steelers in 1969. Hanratty had done fairly well in the last few games of his rookie year, despite the Steelers' losing streak.

Some Steeler fans read Bradshaw's remarks the

wrong way. He was questioned on radio talk shows by listeners who asked him bluntly if he was putting down Hanratty's capabilities. And even when he went to Three Rivers Stadium, the new home of the Steelers that was still under construction when he signed a mock contract for photographers at the 50-yard line, some workers booed him. He looked at the boobirds, who were six stories up, and wanted to say something but didn't. He didn't want to get off on the wrong foot with the fans. And besides, he had nothing against Hanratty or the other quarterback possibilities, Kent Nix and Dick Shiner, both of whom had started games in the past couple of years for the Steelers.

Bradshaw made it clear that he was going to Pittsburgh to help the team. But if sitting the bench in favor of Hanratty would help the team, then he would do that, too.

Actually, most of Pittsburgh looked forward to Bradshaw's appearance. He first visited the city in February and got a loud cheer when he attended a hockey game and was introduced to the crowd of 12,000. Bradshaw didn't sign with the Steelers on that trip, or on another visit to Pittsburgh in March. But he was already finding out what it was like to be a professional. A clothing manufacturer arranged to pay him $100 a day to model some slacks for a retailers convention in Dallas, Texas. "Goll-ee," he said, after accepting the offer, "they give you $100 a day for *that*. For $100 a day, I'd even wear a dress."

The big money would come in April when Terry, with the guidance of lawyer Pugh, signed his official contract. Lots of athletes like to let the word out about how much they are making, especially in this era of big contracts. Such athletes feel it's good for their egos. Terry felt it was nobody's business how much he would make, and made that point clear. But there were no tough bargaining sessions as both sides came to what they felt was a fair agreement.

The addition of Bradshaw to the Pittsburgh roster meant that one more leftover from the previous year's losing team would have to go to make room for him.

Head Coach Chuck Noll, working through Dan Rooney who handled most of the general manager chores, had been busy from the time he joined the Steelers making deals and acquiring the talent he would need to build a winning team.

Though he was not yet 40 years old, he had been in professional coaching since he was 27. Before that, he was a versatile player for Coach Paul Brown on the great Cleveland Browns team. He was well-schooled in coaching and knew something about quarterbacks because he used to be a "messenger guard" for the Browns. A messenger guard was a guard who alternated on every offensive play with another guard. Each alternate would race to the sideline after a play and get another play from Coach Brown, then dash back on the field to give the play to the quarterback to call. Noll also filled in at linebacker one season when the Browns had a shortage at the position due to injuries.

Noll's playing days ended early, but he was quickly snapped up by the San Diego Chargers as an assistant coach. He helped that team develop winning teams in the old American Football League, then joined the Baltimore Colts, where he helped develop more championship squads. In 1969, he got his chance to move up to the head coaching position with the Steelers.

Knowing that a job with the Steelers is not the most secure coaching position in football, Noll went to work to rebuild the team but fast. Within a year, only 10 of his original 40 players were still on the roster.

One of the biggest changeovers came in the off-season before Bradshaw's rookie season. Along with Bradshaw, top receivers Ron Shanklin, Dave Smith and Jon Staggers were taken in the draft. Mel Blount was taken to improve the defense. Noll traded one of his quarterbacks, Dick Shiner, to the New York Giants for John (Frenchy) Fuqua, a flamboyant running back who would give the team some running support. And he added Preston Pearson, acquired in a trade with the Baltimore Colts, to be his other 1970 running back. Pearson had been a little-used player with the Colts because of his inexperience; in college, he played basketball, not football. But Noll liked his potential. Noll also kept a 1968 16th-round draft choice, Rocky Bleier, on the squad despite the fact that he had been wounded in Vietnam and didn't look like a potential pro running back.

In the next couple of years, there would be other wise draft choices and trade decisions that would lead to success for the long downtrodden Steelers. Noll, the man who made the decision to draft Terry Bradshaw rather than trade him, knew what he was doing.

Bradshaw liked Noll, and had faith in him from the start.

"You look at the Steelers and you ask yourself—what does it take?" Terry said. 'I think from talking to Coach Noll and the players that he can be the one to pull them out of it. He's young. He's a real gentleman."

And Noll liked Terry, too, and not just because of his superior potential. If there was one person in Pittsburgh who didn't mind it when the confident country-boy from Louisiana did his bragging, it had to be the coach.

"Doggone straight," Bradshaw would tell his audience, be it fans or sportswriters. "I think I can go up there and make Pittsburgh a winner. If I didn't think so, I would stay home."

It was refreshing talk by a Pittsburgh player, Noll felt. He had heard enough from losers.

6 Making the Team

The trouble with being the No. 1 selection of the entire National Football League draft is that millions of sets of eyes are focused on that one single athlete. The rest of the draftees on the first round have enough pressure, but it comes mostly from the fans in the area of the team that drafts him. "No. 1" is a different case —all football fans have an interest in how he will do.

"People say that being No. 1 is added pressure," Terry Bradshaw said of the situation he was in. "But I don't look at it that way. I've been taught that pressure is only self-made. If I let them bother me, then that's added pressure. But if I can just forget and go on and do the job like I know I can, then I think I'll do all right. I know there's a problem of being No. 1 in the fans' eyes. They may say, 'Well, you're No. 1, you should be able to go out there and star, take them all the way.'"

Going all the way is a task in itself. Asking one player to carry the load is ridiculous. Asking a rookie player to do it is out of the question. But Terry knew that he would have to live with the problem when he joined the Steeler pre-season camp at Latrobe, Pennsylvania.

A more immediate problem for the rookie quarterback centered around his appearance at the annual College All-Star Game in Chicago. The game pits the best collegiate graduates against the previous year's National Football League champions. Most pro teams would rather have their ace rookies at their training camps so that they can accelerate the learning process of becoming pros. But the pro teams are careful about voicing their complaints because the All-Star Game is popular with the fans. Besides, its proceeds are turned over to charities, so it would be selfish of the pro teams to complain too loudly.

The Steelers wanted badly to have Bradshaw at the early workouts particularly because he was a quarterback. New quarterbacks have the most difficult adjustments to make coming out of college. But Terry, along with quarterbacks Mike Phipps of Purdue and Dennis Shaw of San Diego State, were selected for the game, and there was no way, short of injury, that he could get out of it. The All-Star promoters issued Bradshaw a No. 1 jersey, to match his pro draft selection, and sent him out to the workouts along with everyone else.

Coach Chuck Noll did get a promise from All-Star

Coach Otto Graham, his old Cleveland Browns' teammate, that he wouldn't risk Terry aggravating his right thigh, which had been operated on in April. That, plus a case of the flu, kept Terry out of a special Steeler quarterback classroom in early June. As it turned out, Terry went to the All-Star camp, lasted one day, then got the doctor's permission to return home after limping around.

Before long, he was ready to resume workouts with the Steelers in his effort to win the starting job.

A rookie, no matter how much promise and buildup he has, rarely gets a chance to quarterback his first pro team from start to finish in his initial year. When Terry rejoined the Steelers for pre-season drills, one sportswriter pointed out that the last rookie quarterback to hold down a starting job for a full season was Norm Snead, with the Washington Redskins 10 years before. The experience proved to be a disaster for the Redskins and probably the talented Snead, too. Snead had trouble reading the defenses, mixing up his pass and run plays, using his secondary receivers, and so on. The Redskins finished the season dead-last—with a 1-12-1 record.

Since then, such brilliant prospects as Joe Namath of the New York Jets, Bob Griese of the Miami Dolphins and others had found their first-year woes plentiful. Some quarterbacks, such as Heisman Trophy winners Terry Baker of Oregon State, John Huarte of Notre Dame, Steve Spurrier of Florida and Gary Beban of UCLA, tried for years and still didn't adjust. Some never even got a chance because they could not adjust.

"Terry can be great," said his college backfield coach, Mickey Slaughter, "but he'll need time."

Terry wasted no time giving it a good shot, however. And the Steelers responded by giving him every opportunity. He worked hard, even though he started out behind Kent Nix and Terry Hanratty on the Pittsburgh depth chart.

The Steelers' first exhibition game was against the up-and-coming Miami Dolphins. The Florida team built up a 13-0 halftime lead while Bradshaw watched his counterparts handle much of the quarterbacking. In the fourth quarter, though, he took charge and got the Steelers moving. The Dolphins felt they were lucky to get by with a 16-10 victory when it was all over. Terry had completed 9-of-19 passes, and people who saw the game say at least half of his incompletions were dropped because his receivers couldn't handle the fast-moving ball. Terry drove the team downfield for its only touchdown, and showed enough poise to get the head of a pro scouting network to admit, "There aren't many veterans who take command the way he does." "He's going to be a great one," said Don Shula, the Miami coach.

How Terry took charge is a story in itself. As he recalled, "On the second play of my second series everybody came back to the huddle and they were yakking and laughing. Well, doggone, that made me mad, even though I knew they were just testing me to see what I'd do. I don't like to cuss anyone out but I said, 'Let's cut out the damn fooling around and get down to business.' You know, there was quiet in the huddle for the rest of the time I played."

From then on, Bradshaw ran the show during the exhibition season. The team, much to its own surprise, won its last four games in a row. They beat the powerful Minnesota Vikings, 20-13; the New York Giants, 21-6; the Boston (New England) Patriots, 31-3; and the Oakland Raiders, 20-6, in successive weeks. It was the finest pre-season record in Steelers history and Terry was at the controls for most of the games.

He completed 51 percent of his passes for 663 yards and three touchdowns. In one game, he ripped off an 89-yard TD run, only to have it called back because he stepped out of bounds. He made his share of rookie mistakes but more often than not he looked as if he belonged in the starting lineup.

"You can always find out fast about a rookie quarterback," Don Shula said after seeing him play. "You ask him to throw long for accuracy and you ask him to throw those sideline passes. If he can do both well, you know he is special." Shula then went on to recall Bradshaw's pinpoint 65-yard throws and sideline passes "as well as Unitas or Tittle ever threw."

One criticism of Terry during the pre-season games came from a New York Giants front-office executive who said he might not be mean enough. "This kid is still an eagle scout," the critic added. The man changed his tune after Terry led the Steelers to a victory over the Giants.

If Bradshaw were an "eagle scout," his teammates

never noticed it. They responded to his winning attitude, especially when he began patting guys on the back for doing a good job and making sure that the recognition for the victories got shared. Bradshaw established a great relationship with rookie flanker Ron Shanklin, who was quickly becoming his "pet" receiver. But it was the veterans who were his biggest boosters.

"I'm sure he always thought he could win," said starting center Ray Mansfield, a veteran of more than 100 consecutive games with the "old" Steelers.

The pre-season performance earned Terry the opening day assignment in the regular season. The opponent was a so-so Houston Oiler team that hadn't won an opening game in several years. Against them, however, Terry's bubble burst.

The rookie quarterback had a mediocre debut, hitting on only four of 16 passes. One was intercepted. He had trouble finding his receivers and he was pressured by the Oiler line. The result was an embarrassing 19-7 defeat before a home crowd at Pittsburgh. Same old Steelers, many of the fans thought.

Terry earned the respect of his teammates when he took the personal blame for the loss. "We were completely flat and it was my fault. My trouble has come in adjusting to the various zones. I have had some trouble searching instead of reading the opponents. I haven't come off one man to find the open man in a progressive manner." But he was confident as ever.

The next week, at Denver, Bradshaw was back on target, completing half of his 26 passes for a respectable 211 yards. But it was not enough to save the Steelers from a 16-13 defeat. By now, Bradshaw was trying to implant a little confidence into himself as well as his teammates. He admitted he was scared after a miserable first half against the Broncos.

"It wasn't that I was afraid," he said. "It's just a case of knowing now it's for real."

Rookie mistakes come in all forms, but Terry made an unforgivable one the week before the next game against ancient rival Cleveland. A reporter covering the Pittsburgh practice had asked Terry to evaluate the Browns. Terry, with his typical honesty, said he didn't know much about their offense because he hadn't seen their offensive films. But the defense, he said, "isn't a physical defense—it's not overly aggressive, not like the defenses of Oakland and Denver who were pure torture." Terry went on and on, and by the time the team left for Cleveland, the reporter turned in his story.

On Saturday before the game, a big banner headline across the Cleveland *Plain Dealer* sports page read: BRADSHAW EVALUATES BROWNS' DEFENSE: "SMART, NOT OVERLY AGGRESSIVE."

Needless to say, the headline got posted in the Cleveland locker room and the rookie quarterback was on the spot. The fired-up Brown defense stole three of his passes and generally stymied his offense, even though Terry completed 13 of 29 passes for 207 yards. The Browns won the game, and the Steeler losing streak for regular-season games stretched out to 16.

That touched off a series of problems that turned the

bright-eyed rookie sour for most of the rest of his rookie year.

The Steelers did win a game the next week, beating lowly Buffalo, but without much help from Bradshaw, who had a terrible day passing.

His nifty 67-yard pass to batterymate Shanklin resulted in a 7-3 victory over Houston in the following game, but Bradshaw was in trouble again soon after. Noll had a policy of letting the players go their own way after Sunday games, just so they were back at the Pittsburgh practice field on time on Tuesday. Since the Houston game was at Houston, not too far from Terry's Shreveport home, he decided to go home first, then shoot up to Pittsburgh Monday night. But his plane was delayed because of fog, and he didn't reach Pittsburgh until Tuesday night.

During the weekend of the Houston game Terry had missed a team meal and was slapped with a small but significant fine. Now, with his second violation of team rules within a few days, he was in trouble with Coach Noll and the management. The coach was bitter even though Terry had called Monday to inform Noll of his problem. The coach voiced his anger, especially in light of the fact that the Steelers were finally getting on the winning track that he had waited so long to see.

Besides that winning pass, Terry had thrown three interceptions at Houston. In the next game, against the Oakland Raiders, he threw four more, and the Steelers were beaten badly. Terry played only briefly and contributed little as Hanratty led the team to an important Central Division victory over the Cincinnati Bengals.

Bradshaw had done a lot of talking by midseason, but his production was minimal. Most of his comments were the result of his frankness and honesty, and his desire to help out the press. Sometimes, he claimed, he was misquoted when the season began going badly for him. Sometimes it was his own fault.

In an early November game that fans all over the nation had looked forward to all year long—Joe Namath and the Jets versus Terry Bradshaw and the Steelers—both the veteran and the upstart sat the bench. Ironically, the two superarms were tied for the league lead in only one department—interceptions. Each had 12.

Other than that, Terry was next-to-last among the 29 quarterbacks listed in the most recent statistics, and Terry's 41 percent passing efficiency wasn't enough to keep him in the lineup. The Steelers weren't scoring much with him in the lineup, so Hanratty—the home-town favorite—won the starting job back.

Except for leading the team to victory in a rematch with Cleveland a couple of weeks later, there were few bright moments left for the confused "Blond Bomber." Superarm had been defused, his ego deflated. The press became his personal enemy. And many of the fans turned against him, too, when he made a foolish remark saying that he didn't want to play behind the popular Hanratty.

The other Terry had had to fight his way up the ranks to get playing time. He was a Notre Dame graduate, which made him acceptable to the large Catholic population in and around Pittsburgh. And he was a fighter, smaller than Bradshaw but just as feisty. A second-round draft choice, he had to work harder than Bradshaw for everything he got; he just didn't have Bradshaw's natural tools.

So when Bradshaw's comment about not wanting to play behind Hanratty reached the papers, many fans exploded.

Once in late season, when Bradshaw and his mother and brother attended a hockey game at the same arena where he had been cheered so loudly only months before, a large portion of the crowd greeted him with boos.

Bradshaw was the victim of 12 more interceptions before the season was over, bringing his total to 24. Quarterbacks are expected, traditionally, to match their interceptions with touchdown passes. That's one way of blotting those ugly statistics off your record. But for his rookie year, Bradshaw threw for only six TD's. His rushing was impressive (7.3 yards a carry) but virtually unnoticed as the insiders pointed to his 38.1 passing percentage. Good passers should be over 50 percent.

The Steelers could boast that they had improved their record from 1-13 to 5-9 in one year's time. But Bradshaw, the player everyone across the nation was watching was just another quarterback fighting for a job.

"My confidence was completely shot," he said after the season. "I did everything wrong. I got in trouble, missed a plane, popped off to the press. I lost all my confidence that I could throw the ball. I had a lot of growing up to do."

At one point, he said, "The people in Pittsburgh don't like me much."

But he was wrong. He was a young athlete, just turned 22 years old in the middle of the season, with pressure that older quarterbacks probably could not handle. He had to get his game together, and he had to get it together soon. That's all that the fans in Pittsburgh wanted from him.

7 Remaking the Quarterback

The remaking of Terry Bradshaw began almost as soon as the 1970 season ended. It began with a much needed rest and a chance for him to get his mind off football. One of the first things Terry did was to enroll back in Louisiana Tech, so that he could finish his education. He spent his spare moments fishing and relaxing, away from people. And he prepared for his April marriage to Melissa Babish, a former Miss Teenage America whom he had met in Pittsburgh. It was good to be back in Louisiana,

But the key factors that would help him in his future were taking place in Pittsburgh. For one thing, the Steelers put together another remarkable draft under the direction of the Rooney family and Coach Chuck Noll.

The first man picked was Frank Lewis, a lightning fast wide receiver from that great incubator of pro football stars, Grambling College, just down the road from Ruston, where Terry was studying. Lewis, with 4.5-second speed in the 40-yard dash and 9.4 speed in the 100, was a brilliant prospect who had caught 99 passes for 26 touchdowns in his college career. He would have difficulty adjusting to his first season just as No. 1 choice Terry had, but he would play a major role in Terry's future.

Another important choice was tight end Larry Brown of Kansas, who would soon earn a starting job. On the line, the Steelers picked up a fine blocking guard in Gerry Mullins, a fast 240-pounder out of Southern Cal who would earn a starting job before 1971 ended.

The Steelers likewise strengthened themselves on defense, by selecting soon-to-be starters in Jack Ham, linebacker from Penn State; Glen Edwards, defensive back from Florida A&M; Mike Wagner, a safety from Western Illinois; and Dwight White, a fearsome defensive end from Joe Greene's alma mater, North Texas State.

The Steelers also picked up a superb kicker in Roy Gerela, who would play an important role in the drives of Terry's that fell short. Gerela came cheap: the Steelers got him on $100 waivers from the Houston Oilers, who had given up on him.

But as far as Terry was concerned, the most important off-season acquisition was that of quarterback coach Vito (Babe) Parilli, a native of the Pittsburgh

71

area who had recently retired after 16 years as an active player in pro football. Parilli was the 12th leading passer in pro football history, having thrown 178 touchdown passes. He was the Most Valuable Player for the Boston (New England) Patriots in 1963 and had most recently been Joe Namath's backup quarterback with the Super Bowl-winning New York Jets. He was young—just 41—and likeable, and had a great deal of respect for the potential of Terry Bradshaw.

Coach Noll had wanted to hire a quarterback coach for Bradshaw during his rookie year. In fact, he wanted to get Mickey Slaughter, the assistant at Louisiana Tech and a former Denver Bronco starter. But Slaughter turned down the Steelers because of family pressures, and the season was just about to begin so Noll took over the chore himself.

The head coach spread himself too thin, however, and he didn't really have the expertise of a former quarterback. So one of the first things he did when the 1970 season was over was to go on a search for a quarterback coach. He signed Parilli in April 1971.

Though Terry had left Pittsburgh a very discouraged young man at the end of the 1970 season, Parilli found him an eager and willing pupil. Terry had a chance to sit back and study his mistakes, many of which were pointed out to him by The Babe. One of the first things Parilli did after he was hired was arrange a three-hour meeting. The two hit it off fine.

"I think he was fabulous," Terry said about that first get together. "He impressed me with what he knows about passing. I think he's going to help us a lot."

72

Parilli said after that meeting that "Joe Namath is a great quarterback and Terry Bradshaw is going to be a great one. Terry's arm is as good as anyone's anywhere."

Such reassuring words helped Terry regain confidence in himself. He thought back about the pressure that was put on him and decided that he was going to learn from his mistakes, not repeat them.

"I look on that rookie year as definitely up and down," he said. "I certainly don't regret anything that happened. If people asked me if I'd like to have the same year again, the answer would be no. But I wouldn't trade that year because of all the things I learned."

Looking back, Bradshaw's problems were not all of his own making. The whole pass-catching corps (wide receivers and tight ends) were new to professional football, and they had to learn with him. The runners were new to the team, too, so there was the problem of timing on handoffs and knowing where players would be at any given time. And there were times when the blocking had broken down; Terry had been "sacked" by opposing tacklers 25 times.

Before the summer drills began at St. Vincent College in Latrobe, Pennsylvania, Parilli made it a special point to keep Terry from getting down on himself. Rebuilding the youngster's confidence was the first priority in making him a first-class quarterback.

One way to help brace that confidence was to get Terry to cut down on his interceptions. To do so, Parilli began badgering Terry to cut down on the hard throws.

"Lay it in there," the coach would tell him over and over again.

Terry had built himself up physically to 220 pounds in the off-season by lifting weights. But he was gaining strength in his upper body to help him as a runner, not make his passes speed faster. He got a chance to work on Parilli's theories with tight end Dennis Hughes, who joined him in Louisiana.

One other thing that changed in Terry during the off-season was his attitude about not expecting everything good to happen to him right away.

"I expect big things from me this year," he said. "I've got goals. You've got to expect great things. They're going to come, believe me, they are. But it's going to take time.

"I think it's going to take five years for me to step out on that field and feel completely confident that no matter what comes up, I can handle it."

Among his goals were three important ones. One was to cut down the number of interceptions that had got him into so much trouble as a rookie. He and Parilli discussed that often, and Terry was persuaded to cool his blazing hot passes.

The second was to control the ball more. He would try to sustain longer drives, to get his team in position to score more often even if it wouldn't be by touchdown passes. He'd work harder at leading the ground game, and perhaps run the ball more himself when he got caught behind the line while trying to pass.

And the third goal would be to come up with the big play more often. Terry had made some big plays in

1970, but too often he wasn't careful about the timing of the big play and the opponents would be waiting for him.

As Terry packed his bags to leave for Latrobe, where the Steelers held their pre-season drills, he had to wonder how Coach Noll would accept him back. Parilli, after all, was hired to improve Terry Hanratty's game, too. And a third quarterback, Bob Leahy of little Emporia State (Kansas) College, would be joining the team.

Bradshaw could hardly forget that in the closing 1970 game against the Philadelphia Eagles he was used only sparingly and was not allowed to throw a single pass. Much to his surprise, he found his name at the top of the "depth chart" when he arrived at St. Vincent College.

As the drills progressed, teammates began noticing a change in their young quarterback. "There were a lot of things that confused him last year and now you can stand with him back of the huddle at practice and notice the difference," said John Fuqua, the team's leading rusher. "He can call the defenses and he notices things like where the linebackers are moving. He's seeing things he didn't see last year."

Bradshaw, Fuqua and the rest of the Steelers were a well-oiled unit when they took on the Green Bay Packers in the first exhibition game. Terry started the game and the highlight of the day was a 98-yard drive for a touchdown which helped Pittsburgh to a 16-13 victory.

Terry continued to look good in pre-season games. But when the Steelers opened their regular season against the Chicago Bears, he fell back into his old pattern. There were four interceptions and very little yardage gained from his 24 pass attempts.

But Noll continued to have faith in him, and Terry responded by leading the team to victory over the Cincinnati Bengals the following week. It was his best game as a pro. Terry completed 18 passes for 249 yards and two touchdowns—all personal highs in his National Football League career. He only had one interception in 30 attempts.

But the Steelers as a team were showing little improvement. After six games, they had only a 3-3 record.

If Terry had any doubts about his own role on the team at the time, Coach Noll made it clear that Terry was his starting quarterback—no ifs, ands or buts. Terry was hitting over 54 percent of his passes, running the ball well himself and leading the team up and down field. He was beginning to show the promise everyone had predicted.

But when everything was going well, and Terry was ripping off a 39-yard run against the Cleveland Browns near the end of the first half of the eighth game, he injured a leg as he was driven out of bounds. Terry hobbled off the field and was replaced by Terry Hanratty, who protected the 16-0 lead Bradshaw had given the team.

Noll made it quite clear after the game that he was not against Terry running the ball when his judgment called for it. "The only people who try to deter him from running are the opponents," said Noll. "And they don't want him to run for the obvious reason."

Terry had 175 yards rushing at the time, tops for any conference quarterback.

Terry was back in action the following week against the powerful Miami Dolphins and came through with his best game yet. The Dolphins were on their way to the Super Bowl in 1971, but that didn't faze Bradshaw. After Miami took a 3-0 lead, Terry began filling the air with passes. He was mixing short and long passes right from the start against the vaunted Miami defense.

He hit on 10 straight passes at one point and was so hot he made 18 of 19. In the first half, he passed for three touchdowns, two to Dave Smith and one to Ron Shanklin. His Steelers grabbed a 21-3 lead over the stunned Dolphins and 66,000 fans in Miami. Terry continued to throw in the second half and wound up the day 25-for-36, for 253 yards. But the Dolphins' All-League quarterback, Bob Griese, put on a passing display of his own and rallied his team to a 24-21 victory.

But after that, Bradshaw went into a slump and finally was benched in favor of Hanratty in the next-to-last game, against the Bengals. Cincinnati was quickly becoming Pittsburgh's biggest rival in the American Football Conference's Central Division and seemed like the team to beat in the future if the Steelers were ever to get into a division race. Thus Noll wanted a victory badly over his old coach, Paul Brown.

So Hanratty got his first start of the year. But Hanratty suffered a broken collarbone early in the game. Much to Bradshaw's disappointment, Noll replaced Hanratty with Bob Leahy, who had just been brought up from the taxi squad and had never played in a National Football League game. Leahy couldn't rally the Steelers back from a 13-6 deficit.

So Noll went with Bradshaw for the final quarter. Terry got hot and fired a pass to John Fuqua, one that the running back went 40 yards with to score and put the Steelers in the lead again. Then, guiding the team brilliantly down the field, Terry engineered another touchdown drive that was climaxed with a short 5-yard pass to Ron Shanklin. Pittsburgh walked off the field with a 21-13 victory. He had earned his job back as 1971 came to a close.

The Steelers were only 6-8 in the win-loss column for the season but had definitely shown the improvement they desired in the offense. Especially at quarterback, where Terry Bradshaw was looking like a real pro. His passing percentage jumped to 54.4 percent. He more than doubled his touchdowns, to 13, and cut down on his interceptions. He was the best running quarterback in American Conference, having gained 247 yards and scored five TDs.

For 1972 he had something to look forward to. And, unlike his rookie year, he had something to look back upon, too.

8 Championship Bound

There was a "new" Terry Bradshaw who showed up for training camp at Latrobe before the start of the 1972 season. In past seasons he had always sounded confident, cocksure that he'd be the starting quarterback and the man who would lead the Steelers out of the second-division role they had become accustomed to. But, now, in 1972, he was a two-year veteran with many of the mistakes in his past. He had experience, more maturity and a better grasp of what the pro game is all about.

"The first year, you are a rookie and nervous," he said. "The second year you are trying to prove your rookie season wasn't a fluke. Your third year, you say, 'I'll be here for a long time; no one's going to run me out of town.'"

Coach Noll echoed his faith in the third-year quarterback when he said, "For the first time since I've been here, we have quarterbacks (he meant Hanratty, too) who know what the heck they are doing. That's the big difference. It's like night and day."

The rest of the city was beginning to rally around the quarterback and his teammates, too, finally. One veteran newspaperman, Pat Livingston of the Pittsburg *Press,* noticed this as the season got under way. In exhibition games, the Steelers rolled up 56 points in one of their games. In their final pre-season contest, the Steelers tied a sound Minnesota team, 20-20. Then Pittsburgh, behind Terry's running and passing, whipped a good Oakland Raiders team, 34-28, in the opening game of the season at Three Rivers Stadium. Over 51,000 Pittsburgh fans were on hand, and they were delighted. The game was more one-sided than the final score showed, as Terry scored twice and threw a 57-yard touchdown pass to Ron Shanklin to give his team a 34-14 fourth-quarter lead.

The fans cheered openly and loudly for the quarterback they had booed in past years.

But sportswriter Livingston made a lot of sense when he wrote, "As with any quarterback playing before a hometown audience week after week, Bradshaw has been slow to convince the fans of Pittsburgh that he has, indeed, fared well in his race with the calender. Most people are not aware that his rate of development compares favorably with that of Joe Namath in Joe's first three years with the Jets.

"Over a similar span, two full seasons and a pre-season campaign, Namath won 19 games with a solid, veteran-dominated Jet team behind him. Playing mostly with rookie receivers, Bradshaw's Steelers have won 22 games (in a comparative time)."

Livingston added that Terry was merely 24, having just celebrated a birthday, and that his day would come.

The performance in the opening-day game with Oakland earned Terry "Back of the Week" honors from the Associated Press. It was his first honor of any sort in the pros. Terry was somewhat stunned by the honor because he connected on only 7-of-17 passes and had had three of his attempts intercepted. But his running game and leadership had been enough to convince the wire-service panel of experts.

The heated rival Cincinnati Bengals defeated the Steelers in the second game of the season at their stadium on the Ohio River. Terry scored a touchdown—the only one of the day by either team—but the Bengals made five field goals and won, 15-10. A rain-drenched field and some questionable officiating calls hurt the Steelers, who had an apparent Bradshaw-to-Shanklin touchdown pass called back.

In the next two weeks the weather was clearer and Bradshaw filled the air with passes like he'd never done before in the pros. Against the St. Louis Cardinals and the Dallas Cowboys he threw a total of 94 times. A 38-yard pass to the improving second-year man, Frank Lewis, in the final 66 seconds won the game against the Cardinals, but for all his 94 passes that was the only touchdown.

In fact, that pass and a 1-yard quarterback-keeper by Terry in the Cardinal game were the only touchdowns the offense got in those two games. The Steelers were now 2-2 for the season, having beaten St. Louis but lost to Dallas, and it was obvious a more balanced offense would be needed if the team was to improve.

Bradshaw's rapport with his receivers—Dave Smith, Ron Shanklin and to a lesser degree the improving Lewis—was good. And he could hit the running backs for short gains. But he needed a stronger running attack if the Steelers were going to upgrade their standing at a faster pace than one game a year.

In 1971, the two best Steeler rushers had been Frenchy Fuqua, with 625 yards, and Preston Pearson, with 605. Those were not very impressive figures, so the Steelers went for a big strong running back in the draft. The Steelers did not get to draft until 12 other teams had made their first-round choices, but when their turn came around a big, fast back named Franco Harris from Penn State was still available. Harris had gotten little publicity in college because he teamed with Lydell Mitchell, a smaller back but a game-breaking All-America. But Noll liked Harris's size and strength and speed. Franco was 6′ 2″ tall and weighed about 230 pounds.

Harris started the season slowly but by game five, against the Houston Oilers, he broke loose for 115 yards. Terry mixed up Franco's 19 attempts with seven carries of his own and far less passing. Harris scored once, Bradshaw scored once and Lewis grabbed one of Terry's passes in the end zone. Meanwhile the young Steelers' defense had become rock-ribbed and held the

Oilers in check. Pittsburgh won an impressive 24-7 victory.

Fuqua rushed for 111 yards the next game against New England; then Harris came back with games of 100 or more the following two weeks against Buffalo and Cincinnati.

By then, the Steelers were riding a four-game winning streak, something they had not accomplished since 1957, and the whole city was getting excited. The improved running game, which was aided by Terry's guiding hand, perked up the entire team. Bradshaw began throwing less, but just as effectively.

In fact, in the fourth game of that victory streak against the Bengals, Cincinnati was looking for the run so much that Terry tossed three touchdown passes —two of them to Lewis—and the Steelers won, 40-17. The victory pushed the Steelers one game ahead of the Cleveland Browns in the Central Division standings and the whole National Football League was becoming aware of the young Pittsburgh team.

The defense, nicknamed "the Steel Curtain" after a radio station held a contest to choose a suitable name for tackle Joe Greene and his ball-hungry pursuers, was playing brilliantly, too. The Steelers had become a "team" in the truest sense of the word.

A pair of fourth-period fumble recoveries by one of those defenders, young linebacker Jack Ham, played the key role in a victory over Kansas City the next week, to bring the winning streak to five. Harris got his 100 yards again. Pittsburgh was now 7-2 for the season and a definite championship contender with a big game against the Browns coming up.

The Steelers lost that game to the Browns, 26-24, before a crowd of 83,000 in Cleveland when Don Cockroft kicked a 26-yard field goal in the final eight seconds. Harris had romped again, including a 75-yard touchdown run that put the Steelers ahead in the final quarter. And while the Steelers lost and fell into a divisional tie with the Browns, they felt confident about the future.

The next week, the Steelers went out and whipped the powerful Minnesota Vikings, again depending upon the run. But it was two plays by Terry—a 1-yard touchdown run and a 17-yard pass to Lewis—that clinched the game, 23-10, in the final period.

It was Terry's seventh touchdown run of the season. He, too, was enjoying the fruits of the Steelers' new ground attack. But so was everyone. Frenchy Fuqua, in 11 games, had already gained almost as many yards as the season before when he was the team's first-ranked runner. Now playing a secondary role to Harris, who had over 100 yards again, Fuqua was producing more effectively.

As the team prepared for another showdown, and the most important one in 1972, with the Cleveland Browns, Terry took time to discuss the change in his role with the team.

"In my first two years, the offense was built around the pass," he analyzed. "But the way Franco and Frenchy have been running and the way we've been winning, we have to adjust our passing plans. All my life, my play-calling has been geared to the pass and I never really understood the running game. But with these guys, you just have to run the ball."

The coaching staff did not mind. They had achieved what they wanted—a balanced attack in which Bradshaw's strong arm could be used as a surprise, not a normal every-play weapon. Bradshaw himself was the third-best runner on that team and was averaging more yards per carry than his backfield mates. He would end the season with 346 yards and an even 7-yard average per carry, both figures being tops in the American Football Conference. He said he didn't like to run if he didn't have to, but just the threat of him doing so added pressure to opposing linebackers.

In the showdown with the Browns, Terry threw only 17 passes, a marked contrast to the year before when he had averaged about 30 passes for his full games. Meanwhile, the Steelers ran the ball 43 times.

From the time Terry manuevered the team into field goal position for Roy Gerela in the first quarter, the game belonged to the Steelers. Gerela put the Steelers ahead, 3-0, and Harris made it 10-0 with a 1-yard plunge in the second period. It was Harris again in the third period with an 11-yard scoring run and he was on his way to another 100-yard plus effort.

It would make his sixth straight 100-yard day, tying an all-time record set by the great Jim Brown of the Cleveland Browns, which was pretty good for a rookie who was late earning a starting job with the Steelers.

Then, in the fourth period, with the Browns still scoreless, Terry made use of his selective passing scheme. The Browns were completely off guard when he lofted a pass to rookie tight end John McMakin. McMakin grabbed the ball and raced 78 yards for a touchdown.

Pittsburgh scored two more times on field goals and completely demolished Cleveland, 30-0, for one of the biggest victories in Pittsburgh history. The team stood alone on the top of the Central Division standings with just two games to go.

"I never thought I'd like playing for a running team," said Terry afterward, "but I really do. With Franco and Frenchy in there, I have more time to throw."

Terry got hurt in the next game, suffering a dislocated shoulder, but the Steelers defense held tight and kept Houston from scoring a touchdown.

In the final game of the regular season, Terry came back to lead the team to a 24-2 blasting of San Diego. Though the Steelers were now entrenched as a ground team going into the playoffs for the first time, it was ironic that their last TD of the regular season was one familiar to Pittsburgh fans in the previous two seasons —a pass from Bradshaw to Shanklin.

There wasn't a happier group of fans in pro football than the 50,350 who showed up at Three Rivers Stadium on a warm, clear 43-degree Christmas weekend day to watch the Steelers play in their first championship-style game. The team had just finished its regular season with an 11-3 record, easily the best in the team's history. The offense, sparked by Bradshaw and the runners, had scored 343 points—a team record. And the "Steel Curtain" defense had given up only 175 points, second best among all National Football League teams; only the unbeaten Miami Dolphins, who had allowed 171 points, did better.

The opponent for the Steelers in the semi-final game for the American Football Conference would be the Oakland Raiders, whom the Steelers had upset in the season opener. The Raiders were led by quarterback Daryle Lamonica, a 10-year veteran who had averaged two touchdown passes a game for the past six seasons. In 1972, he had thrown for 18, far better than Terry's 12.

As it turned out, neither quarterback got anywhere against the opposing team's defense as a scoreless first half unraveled. But Pittsburgh's defense was clamping down harder and Terry kept the Steelers in the game with a careful, ball-control offense. It was a rock-'em, sock-'em football game that was typical of those earliest Steelers teams of the 1930s.

Pittsburgh finally got on the scoreboard well into the third quarter when a Steeler drive came to a halt and Roy Gerela kicked an 18-yard field goal. Gerela booted another three-pointer in the fourth quarter, and the two teams went into the final four minutes of play with Pittsburgh ahead, 6-0.

By that time the frustrated Raiders had given up on Lamonica and replaced him with young Ken Stabler. Stabler marched the Raiders 50 yards downfield to the Steeler 30. Then, as the Pittsburgh defense blitzed him, Stabler snaked his way through the Steeler line and raced 30 yards for the game's first touchdown. Nobody touched him. George Blanda kicked the extra point and the Raiders led the listless Steelers, 7-6.

The Steelers had to turn to the passing game now. It was Bradshaw versus that mean, veteran-laden Oakland defense. And it was Bradshaw against the clock. There were only 73 seconds left.

Terry and the Steelers were having a particularly rough time against Raider defensive back Jack Tatum. In the first half, he had clobbered Franco Harris with a fourth-down tackle when the Steelers were trying for their first score. Now, in the waning minutes of the game, he was batting down Terry's desperation passes.

There was time for only one more play, and the Steelers were 60 yards away from paydirt when Terry dropped back for one more try. Superarm would have to be at his best. Since his regular receivers were covered closely, all day, and since the Oakland defense had dropped back to guard against the bomb, Terry spotted Frenchy Fuqua in the open about 25 yards downfield. He drilled the ball at him. But the pesky Tatum was there again and batted the ball before Fuqua could get a grasp of it.

The ball began descending to the turf after Tatum hit it; if it reached the ground the game would be over. Suddenly, out of nowhere, Franco Harris, who had been trailing Fuqua, picked up the ball only inches off the ground and began roaring toward the Raider goal line 42 yards away. Franco poured on the steam as the befuddled Raiders were stunned, thinking they had a victory wrapped up. Harris made it all the way. Bradshaw had a 60-yard touchdown pass to his credit, and the Steelers had one of the most incredible victories ever recorded in pro football history! The Steelers left the field with a 13-7 triumph.

That same weekend the Miami Dolphins stretched their winning to 15 in the other American Conference playoff game. They would be a solid favorite to beat the "Miracle Steelers," and their hopes were strengthened further when Terry wound up in the hospital with a severe case of flu the week before the game. He spent two nights hospitalized, but managed to be back on the field on the final day of 1972 when Pittsburgh took on the Dolphins.

The game was only minutes old when bad luck felled Bradshaw again. Terry had driven the Steelers toward the Dolphin goal line in the first quarter, and as he neared the end zone he called for a keeper play.

Bradshaw almost made it in but was hit hard by Miami's All-Pro safety Jake Scott and fumbled. As Terry came down hard on his shoulder, the ball trickled into the Dolphin end zone. Luckily Steeler lineman Gerry Mullins fell on it for a touchdown. The Steelers had a 7-0 lead.

But the play cost the Steelers their quarterback. Terry tried running the team on a series of downs shortly after that but was so shaken by the flu and the contact with Scott that he had to leave the game. He couldn't remember the game plan, and it didn't even help when the coaches tried to explain things to him on the sideline.

"I was pretty looney," he recalled later.

Hanratty replaced Bradshaw, and while he kept the Steelers in contention for a while the Dolphins' time-consuming offense put Miami out in front and began eating up the clock.

With Miami ahead, 21-10, in the final seven minutes, Bradshaw had revived enough to go back into the game. He marched the Steelers 71 yards on just four plays, the last one being his 12-yard pass to Al Young for a touchdown. But there wasn't enough time after that, and the Dolphins killed all hopes by picking off a couple of his passes.

It was a sad way to end such a successful season.

But Terry, the eternal optimist, said before packing up his gear and returning home, "I've had three years now—one of frustration, one where I've learned to pass and one of learning how to run the ball. Maybe next year I can learn to do them all together and then I'll be able to drive 'em all crazy."

9 Losing the Job

If Terry thought he was going to sit back and enjoy the off-season for a change, he was wrong. Before he left Pittsburgh after the 1972 playoffs, he spoke casually about how the pressure was off him.

The Steelers' success with the running game had relieved him of the responsibility of being the main man on *every* play. The interceptions had been few and far between in 1972; in fact, he ranked about the league's best in low percent of passes stolen. And on top of everything, leading the team to its finest season in nearly four decades should have said something about the job he was doing.

But before the 1973 training camp opened, a story appeared in a Miami newspaper in which Dolphins quarterback Bob Griese evaluated the quarterbacks in the league. Griese spoke about Bradshaw's potential and raw talent, but he stung Terry personally with some remarks about the way he got ready for games.

"All Terry needs to do is prepare a little bit more for a game," Griese was quoted as saying. "Reading defenses in the thick of a game is real hard. You can relieve this by your preparation during the week. I mean, watching films, studying the defense. It gets to where you can almost expect a certain coverage at a certain time, and it cuts down your job of reading defense. Terry should watch more films so he knows more of what to expect."

Terry had been hearing petty criticisms ever since he had come into the National Football League. But this one hurt; it came from a fellow player—and one who had not seen Terry play all that much. In fact, Terry had done considerably well against the Dolphins the few times he faced them.

That criticism, along with the growing gripes of Pittsburgh fans and some backhanded comments by the media, began gnawing at Bradshaw. It didn't help, either, when Coach Noll pulled him out of a 1973 exhibition game after he gave up three second-quarter interceptions to the New York Giants and bawled him out on the sidelines.

After the game was over, Noll was quoted as saying, "Our problem is that we played dumb offense . . . Bradshaw didn't move the team. He was nowhere close to his potential."

The word "dumb" kept cropping up more and more in 1973 as Steeler fans expected more and more from the 25-year-old quarterback. Never mind that Bradshaw was way ahead of schedule in producing victories. The Namaths, the Dawsons, the Jurgensens, the Unitases had not even come close to matching Terry's success at a comparable age. What hurt most, however, was the word "dumb."

"What do you have to be to throw a pass—an Albert Einstein?" Terry asked one day. "I'm sure I know as much as any other quarterback. If I'm stupid, I guess a lot of us are."

One other problem was that the Steelers had three good young quarterbacks—and each had his own following.

Hanratty was still the darling of many of the fans. Joe Gilliam, a young strong-arm thrower, was the darling of the black fans, who thought the Steelers were holding him back because of his color. Bradshaw had his following, too, but it wasn't that vocal.

The Steelers continued their 1972 success into the new season with Bradshaw at the controls. After four games, they had scored 131 points and were the only unbeaten team left in the American Conference. Then Terry hit upon bad times. The Cincinnati Bengals upset the Steelers, 19-7, and the New York Jets were leading the Steelers, 14-12, until Hanratty pulled the game out in the fourth period. An important rematch with Cincinnati was coming up next, and the Steelers' fans were riding Bradshaw mercilessly.

The second Bengal game, like most Cincy-Pittsburgh contests, promised to be a rugged one physically for both teams. Early in the game Bradshaw was intercepted en route to the goal line, and was booed loudly.

The next time he got the ball, he was trying a quarterback sneak to pick up some needed yardage and he crashed into one of the Bengals' giant tackles, 6' 6", 265-pound Steve Chomyszak. Chomyszak clobbered him, and then fell over Terry as he completed his tackle. Terry landed on his shoulder and hurt it badly. As he started to get up, there was the possibility of a broken collarbone.

Bradshaw had hardly risen to his feet, holding his suffering right shoulder and limping, when a good portion of the fans at Three Rivers Stadium began to cheer —*cheer,* not boo. They were happy to see Bradshaw hurt, even though he was the quarterback of their team. Even though he was obviously in pain. It was a low point in the history of Pittsburgh sports.

Some players came to the defense of Terry.

"It was vicious," said Mean Joe Greene, the 275-pound All-Pro tackle who would have liked to get his hands on some of the fans. "He needs to know he's our quarterback and that this team is behind him, and it is. . . . People don't realize that something like that could affect his whole career."

Terry Hanratty, who inherited Terry's job for four weeks while he's recovering, told one fan who said he cheered when Bradshaw went out: "You're sick!"

Bradshaw tried not to show his bitterness over the situation as he recuperated. But he couldn't help but say something.

"If you don't block them out of your mind," he said about the boobirds, "you go batty. All I care about is the rapport I have with our players and coaches. It makes no difference to me one way or the other what the fans think. I've decided that I just have to take a downright rough, tough kind of approach and say the heck with them."

The worst part about the fans, and especially some of the younger ones, is that they would make their remarks right to Terry's face. "Hey, Bradshaw, you stink," he'd hear. Others would make remarks to his teammates, such as, "If he's so smart, why couldn't he get into Louisiana State?"

"Before I knew what hit me, I had been hung with a national image of a big, dumb, small-college, rural, Southern, Bible-totin' kid who had a strong arm and not enough sense to come in out of the rain. A hick, that's what they thought of me—a hick."

The Steelers won a couple of games with Hanratty in the lineup, then went into a two-game tailspin. Hanratty, too, got hurt, and was replaced by Joe Gilliam.

It was in a game against Miami, when the Steelers were suffering a third straight setback, that Bradshaw made his comeback. The score was 20-0, Dolphins, and Gilliam could do nothing. Terry got into the lineup and began firing strikes through the Miami zone defense and got back two touchdowns. Nobody is supposed to throw into a zone and survive, but Terry's passes were so hard and so accurate it didn't matter.

Bradshaw then led the team to impressive victories in the last two games of the season and got the team into the playoffs again. In a playoff rematch with the

Raiders at Oakland, the Steelers didn't fare well, despite Terry's two touchdown passes. And another season came to an end.

It hadn't been a pleasant one, because of the boobirds, the injuries, the disappointing ending. In the off-season, there would be a divorce, too, that would complicate Terry's problems. He was maturing, but maturing the hard way. And he was becoming more tough minded.

In the off-season, he seriously thought of joining the new World Football League. His contract with the Steelers was still in effect, but the New York Stars of the WFL, coached by his old friend Babe Parilli, had made him a lucrative offer. The idea of being associated with Parilli, who had done so much to help him develop as a pro, seemed interesting.

But in late May he worked out terms with the Steelers again. "I didn't like the idea of playing in small stadiums, ones that might not be filled," he said. "And I still want to take the Steelers to the Super Bowl." His lawyer added that the new contract was a good one: "Terry Bradshaw will be the grand old man of the NFL by the time this contract expires."

Money aside, Terry's 1974 problems continued because the National Football League's player union went on strike, thus delaying his start in the pre-season drills. The late start didn't help him, and Joe Gilliam was already becoming the man the Steelers wanted to see more of in the early drills.

Gilliam's passes were the talk of the camp at Latrobe. Meanwhile, Bradshaw nursed nagging arm injuries while Gilliam got in more and more playing time in exhibition games.

There loomed a possibility of a two-quarterback system, in which Gilliam would play the first half of regular-season games and Bradshaw would come in for the second half. Bradshaw was completely opposed to such an idea.

"It ruins a team," he said. As that idea was discarded and it became more and more of a possibility of Bradshaw being the No. 2 quarterback, Terry hinted that he wanted to be traded.

As the season neared, Gilliam monopolized the playing time in exhibition games. He completed 60 percent of his throws, many for long yardage, and tossed 11 touchdown passes as the Steelers won all six of their games.

Bradshaw, meanwhile, played little and began figuring that Gilliam was going to get the No. 1 job.

"I've never been in this situation before," Terry said. "I've always been No. 1. I know you start the guy who is producing, and Joe's producing." His own arm was hurting, but he admitted it got better and better the more Gilliam performed.

Still, on opening day, it was Gilliam, not Bradshaw, in the starting role. And Terry Hanratty at one point passed up Bradshaw for the backup job. Hanratty was the second quarterback used in the opening game against Baltimore after Gilliam passed for 257 yards and two touchdowns. Bradshaw didn't even play.

"Joe's had the hot hand," said Bradshaw. "But the time will come when we have to establish a running threat. My style is ball control and I'll wait until this thing runs its course."

The "thing" ran its course longer than Bradshaw expected. With Gilliam at the helm, Pittsburgh posted a 4-1-1 record. But in his sixth game, Joe connected on only 5-of-18 passes against the Cleveland Browns and the Steelers narrowly eked out a 20-16 victory. The Steelers had been winning all right, but not impressively. And the opposition so far was not strong.

A game with the Atlanta Falcons, who had a tight-knit defense, was coming up on Monday night television. The week before the game, Coach Noll asked Bradshaw if he would be ready to go all the way. But Noll didn't make up his mind for certain until just before the game. He told the surprised Steelers that Terry would start.

"I made the change because of Atlanta's pass rush," said Noll. "You can't just drop back and throw against that type of team. We wanted to play fundamental football."

The result was that Terry, while not passing too effectively, did accomplish what Noll sought. Terry hit on only 9 of 20 passes, but Franco Harris romped for 141 yards in 28 carries—both personal highs for his pro career. Rocky Bleier, playing the other running back, had 78 yards.

As for the crowd at Three Rivers Stadium that night, Terry admitted he heard a few rumbles. But he heard more cheers than boos. It didn't matter either way, however, because he was back in the lineup and that's all he wanted.

10 Who's at Quarterback?

The quarterbacking job was Terry's again, but only as long as he played well. The Steelers had seven games under their belt and in the first six of them, Terry had played a total of one minute. No one could say that his job was secure just because of the good, solid performance in the seventh game. But he would be the starter against the Philadelphia Eagles as the Steelers hoped to keep their hold on first place in the Central Division.

The fact that the Steelers were carrying three quarterbacks of separate individual skills but fairly equal overall abilities kept Coach Chuck Noll and the three quarterbacks on their toes. Noll was forever being asked about how he planned to use his quarterbacks, and he tried his best to evade an answer.

After all, he had to keep all three happy because he did not know when he would have to call upon any one of them. In some ways he was encouraged because the three made for good competition among themselves. On the other hand, though, the team had a real opportunity to go far in the post-season games, and it was important to establish a leader in that all-important position.

As Bradshaw himself would say during the dragout battle for a starting job. "We've got three good quarterbacks, but we've got to get it straightened out. Let's just give the ball to one of them and get going."

The quarterbacks had to be careful about what they said, too, because they did not want to offend each other. All three were smart enough to know a Super Bowl goal was what everyone was shooting for. Visitors to the Steeler locker room were amazed to find that Bradshaw and Gilliam had their lockers right next to each other. It became embarrassing at times when sportswriters would be interviewing one about his opinion of the starting role while the other was standing there getting dressed.

But the quarterbacks kept their cool and didn't rub each other the wrong way despite the rivalry. After Bradshaw engineered the victory over Atlanta, with great help from the running backs, Gilliam only shook his head and remarked, "We were getting eight or ten yards a pop from our backs tonight. And the linemen were coming off the ball and kicking butts. It was fun, I just wished I'd been in there."

But it had been Bradshaw at the controls in the most recent victory and it would be him again at the helm against the Eagles.

Terry proved the coach's judgment correct by guiding the Steelers to another victory. He passed eight yards to Frank Lewis for a first-period touchdown, connected on over half of his other 21 passes and ran for 48 yards. The final score was 27-0 and Terry even got the game ball.

The next week, however, he fell into his old pattern against the Cincinnati Bengals, who were pushing the Steelers for first place in the Central Division. Terry completed only 13 of 35 passes and the running game sputtered as he filled the air with poorly aimed throws. Worse yet, when he could have guided the Steelers into at least a tie in the tight 17-10 game, he threw an interception on one drive, and spoiled another with an incompletion, a sack and a 1-yard loss on a keeper play in a series of plays down near the Bengals' goal line.

Meanwhile, Cincinnati's young quarterback, Ken Anderson, throwing short passes to sustain drives, connected on 16 consecutive passes at one point to break a National Football League record. He had 20 of 22 completions for the game (90.9 percent) to set another record.

The lack of performance won Bradshaw a spot back on the bench in the next game against the Cleveland Browns. The game was scheduled at Cleveland's Municipal Stadium where the Steelers hadn't won a game in 10 years, and Terry Hanratty was awarded the starting role by frustrated Coach Noll.

Hanratty led the team to a touchdown in the first quarter, his two pass completions to Ron Shanklin being the key plays. But he didn't complete another pass in the game. He was only 2-for-15. Still, the Steeler defense, led by Joe Greene, kept the team out in front.

Greene scored on an interception in the first half, then scooped up a fumble and latereled it to defensive back J. T. Thomas for another touchdown. With the game safely tucked away, Joe Gilliam replaced Hanratty and his performance was only mediocre. Noll's quarterback question was more confused than ever.

With all three of his quarterbacks playing poorly, Noll settled on the simplest plan of attack for the upcoming Monday night game against the New Orleans Saints. He would go with his most experienced man, who happened to be Bradshaw. But Noll did not announce his choice.

Noll got some unexpected support in making his decision, which didn't exactly make him happy. The Pittsburgh *Post-Gazette* began running a poll among local sports fans as to who should start. Almost 3,500 fans voted. They gave Bradshaw 41 percent of their votes, Hanratty 32 percent and Gilliam 20 percent. They also showed some humor by giving votes to such "quarterbacks" as Howard Cosell, Raquel Welch, Bobby Layne and Coach Noll himself. One voter explained that he voted for Noll because he thought the old messenger guard of the Cleveland Browns ought to still be sending in the plays.

The poll only made Noll more silent about his choice of quarterback for the New Orleans game. He didn't even bother to tell the players until game time neared. Meanwhile, Terry Hanratty decided to get some revenge on the *Post-Gazette* by running a poll of his own in the Pittsburgh *Press*. Hanratty paid $272 for an advertisement on the sports page asking the readers to select their favorite sportswriter on the *Post-Gazette*.

Bradshaw, somewhat surprised by the support he had got from the Pittsburgh fans he thought were against him for years, responded by going out and playing the best game of his professional career. Before a national television audience that Monday night, he fired a 31-yard scoring pass to Frank Lewis in the first period, ran 18 yards for a touchdown in the second quarter and passed to tight end Larry Brown for a third touchdown in the third period. The touchdown run came right after Terry had a TD pass to Franco Harris called back because of a penalty.

What made Bradshaw's performance in a 28-7 victory so outstanding was not his passing but his running—and his running of the team. Terry gained 99 yards himself in nine carries. He smartly carried the ball himself into gaps left by the Saints' tight defense that was meant to curtail his passing. He also kept Harris on the move, giving him the ball 19 times for another 114 yards.

The post-game locker room was a noisy, happy one for the Steelers, and visitors got the feeling that the team felt it might have finally straightened out the quarterback problem. Bradshaw had not only looked like a technician that night, he looked like a leader. That's what the team needed most from its befuddled three-quarterback system. Noll wouldn't admit that the problem was solved, but he gave that impression. The

Steelers had a two-and-a-half game lead over the Cincinnati Bengals with just three games to play, including one with the Bengals themselves. It was an envious position for a coach to be in.

The Steelers dropped their next game to the Houston Oilers when Bradshaw got sacked badly and had to leave the game early with bruised ribs. But he came back the following week to lead the team to victory over the New England Patriots, to wrap up the divisional championship, and he threw two touchdown passes to help defeat Cincinnati in the regular-season finale. For the third year in a row, he would be the quarterback taking the Pittsburgh Steelers into the post-season playoffs no matter who started what games during the season.

Statistically, Terry's fifth regular season was just about his worst. He passed for only seven touchdowns and threw only 148 times. His 45.3 percent completion rate wasn't anything to boast about. And his overall performance, as rated by a series of statistics the National Football League uses to determine its passing champion, was only 13th among American Conference passers. Even Joe Gilliam ranked above him. Bradshaw's rushing performance, despite, the 99-yard game, was down from his usual yardage, too.

But he had come into his own as a leader in the second half of the 1974 season, and that's what the Steelers wanted from him in the upcoming playoffs.

"The Bradshaw the whole world thinks it knew, that's all over," said Joe Greene, the team's unquestionable defensive leader. "He's been trying to find himself—and he has."

The Steelers' opening playoff game was scheduled for Three Rivers Stadium in Pittsburgh and the team got a break when it drew the Buffalo Bills. The Bills were a "wild card" team—that is, a second-place team with the best record other than divisional leaders.

But the Bills, led by halfback O. J. Simpson and an improved quarterback in Joe Ferguson, were expected to be formidable foes. Ferguson's good season was a surprise to the American Conference. Ironically, he had come from the same high school in Shreveport that produced Bradshaw. The Steelers would be keeping a close watch on him because they could not expend their whole effort trying to bottle up the elusive Simpson.

Terry could not be too concerned with the Buffalo offense, however. The Buffalo defense was all he had on his mind. And then he made it a point only to study the Bills, not to worry about them. His thinking was, if he concerned himself too much about his role and responsibility, he'd have less time to think about the job at hand. It was one of the first times in his pro career that he took that attitude. "I just want to let things roll," he said. "I want to stay on an even keel. I think that comes from not playing. It gives you a sense of awareness."

If Bradshaw had ever been more cool than he was that week before the Buffalo game, he never showed it. Come December 22 and the Steelers' quarterback had everything under control.

The Steelers scored first on a field goal by Roy Gerela, but the Bills came back with a touchdown on a pass by Joe Ferguson to his tight end. Simpson was being stopped by the "Steel Curtain," but the Pittsburgh team was shaken by the Ferguson touchdown.

Bradshaw refused to be rattled, though.

When the Steelers got the ball late in the first period, he began to go to work. Beginning on his own 37-yard line, Terry began to mix his passes and runs with the precision of a computer. As he moved downfield and got temporarily stalled on a third-down-and-8 situation, he ran the ball himself for 12 yards and picked up the needed first down. Then he threw 27 yards to halfback Rocky Bleier for the touchdown early in the second quarter on the same drive. Nine plays, 63 yards and the Steelers were back in front.

On the next series of downs, Bradshaw guided the Steelers 66 yards in seven plays for another touchdown. One of his calls was an end-around to Lynn Swann and two of them were important short pass plays. Franco Harris plunged in for the touchdown.

Still in the second quarter, Bradshaw got yet another drive going. This one, helped along by his passes to Bleier and Swann, lasted only four plays and resulted in another TD for Harris. Then, with 16 seconds left in the half, Bradshaw steered the Steelers into the end zone one more time—their fourth TD in the period. That touchdown, too, saw Terry mixing passes and runs and loking as good as he ever had. The Bills were now down, 29-7, and psychologically beaten.

Terry came out of the game with 4:17 minutes remaining and was met with a loud cheer from the 48,000 fans at Three Rivers. If a vote had been taken then and there for the quarterback job, Bradshaw undoubtedly would have received 100 percent of support. He had run the team brilliantly. "Our offense probably was the best so far this year," said Noll later, who would have no trouble picking a starting quarterback for the American Football Conference championship game a week later with the Oakland Raiders.

Bradshaw himself was pleased. "I never felt so much in control," he told a reporter as the team prepared for Oakland. "What I pride myself about most, though, is that I've been able to come back."

There were still four Super Bowl hopefuls—two in the American Conference, two in the National Conference—as the Steelers got ready to play the Raiders for the third straight season in post-season play. The Raiders had shut out Joe Gilliam and the Steelers early in the 1974 season and the oddsmakers felt this factor, along with the strengths of the two National Conference teams (Minnesota and Los Angeles) made the Steelers the least likely team to go all the way. Against Oakland, Pittsburgh was rated a touchdown underdog.

The Raiders, some experts said, were just too smart for the Steelers. In a way, this was just another slam at Terry and the bringing up of the "dummy" theory again. But Bradshaw and his teammates weren't buying the criticism this time around.

"He just ignores the criticism," said center Ray Mansfield, the grand old man of the offensive line. "If there was anything our offense needed, it was his leadership. He just seems a lot more mature these days. He acts very confident in the huddle."

The Raider game at Oakland should have crunched the "dummy" talk once and for all.

For three periods, the Steelers and Raiders banged heads in a tough defensive battle. The score was only 7-6, Oakland, after 45 minutes of play. But Bradshaw had kept the team in the game with a dazzling selection of plays that enabled the Steelers to retain their field position, and the ball. The Raiders had the ball for only 16 of those 45 minutes. Much to the surprise of the Raiders, who had spread its defense wide to prevent Terry's short game from working, Bradshaw kept the opponents guessing with his switching of plays—call "audibles"—at the line of scrimmage just before the snap of ball. It takes a smart quarterback to call the right "audibles," especially against a veteran team such as Oakland's.

Actually, the Steelers should have had a good lead going into the fourth period. But an official's questionable call nullified a touchdown pass by Bradshaw, and Gerela missed a short field goal after Bradshaw manuevered the team into position.

But Terry refused to be disturbed. Then in the final period he took the Steeler attack right into the heart of the Oakland defense. Throwing short passes and making use of his running tandem of Franco Harris and Rocky Bleier, Terry got the team to rally for three last-period touchdowns. Harris got two of them on runs and the other was the result of a pass from Bradshaw to

Swann. For the full game, only Bradshaw, Harris and Bleier touched the ball in the Steeler backfield.

"Our game plan was to take it right at them," Terry explained. "We planned to run the ball, and our offensive line just blew those guys out. We should have scored more. I probably could have thrown better but I wanted to use the pass as a control weapon, not as a big gun."

As a result of his play selection, the Steelers wound up a 23-13 victor and the American Conference champions. They were on their way to the Super Bowl—just as Terry's dad had predicted five years before. And the person they said made it all possible was Bill Bradshaw's son.

11　Killing the "Dummy" Image

Just before the post-season playoffs began Terry
Bradshaw began sprouting a very reddish beard. Despite that, and his thining hair, he was only 26 years
old as he prepared his team for the Super Bowl. But
someone made the remark that the beard, which Terry
was determined to let grow until the Steelers' winning
ways came to an end, was appropriate because he was
becoming one of the "old men" on the Pittsburgh
squad.

Strangely enough, this was true. The Steelers would
be taking the youngest team ever into the nine-year-old
Super Bowl and five-year veteran Bradshaw was one of
the old-timers on his team.

Forty-two of the 47 Steeler players eligible for the
Super Bowl had been in the league for six seasons or
less. A total of 15 of them were rookies. Only eight had

joined the team before Bradshaw did. Almost the whole offensive team, except for center Ray Mansfield, had spent merely three to six seasons in the National Football League. The same went for the defense, whose only long-term veteran was linebacker Andy Russell.

The bearded wonder Bradshaw, who had let his whiskers grow for almost three weeks before the Super Bowl, would be only the second quarterback ever to lead his team to the Super Bowl with but five years' experience. The other was Joe Namath in 1969.

Contrasted with the Minnesota team, Bradshaw and the Steelers were very young to be participating in pro football's glamour event. Sixteen of the Vikings had played in three Super Bowls each. Only one Steeler—Preston Pearson, the backup halfback—had been to a Super Bowl, as a member of the Baltimore Colts, and then he didn't start.

Bradshaw, who had only thrown 50 touchdown passes in his regular-season games, would be matched against Fran Tarkenton, who had thrown 266 scoring strikes, more than any professional quarterback except Johnny Unitas. And if Bradshaw were a fine runner, Tarkenton was the master scrambler in recent pro football history. And Tarkenton had Super Bowl experience, going back one season when his Vikings lost to the Dolphins.

In most of the previous eight Super Bowls older quarterbacks were at the helm for both the winning and losing teams. The Super Bowl historical highlights are dotted with the achievements of veterans such as Bart Starr of Green Bay, Len Dawson of Kansas City,

Johnny Unitas of Baltimore, Roger Staubach of Dallas and Bob Griese of Miami. Even the losers' quarterbacks—Minnesota's Joe Kapp and Washington's Bill Kilmer—had a ton of pro football experience behind them when they took their teams into the big game.

But despite this knowledge, the Steelers were made the favorites for the January 12, 1975, game with the Vikings. That must have come as a surprise to the Steelers, who only weeks before had been rated the slimmest possibility of going all the way among the four American and National Conference finalists.

The hot hand and sound guidance of Bradshaw had made the difference, though, according to most predictors. The powerful Pittsburgh and Minnesota defenses almost canceled each other out, and both teams had bullish running attacks. The oddsmakers liked the fact that Bradshaw had played so well in the stretch, connecting on 60 percent of his passes in his last four games, including the two playoff contests.

No matter what the oddsmakers said, however, Terry could not get away from the sportswriters and sportscasters who wanted to play up the "dummy quarterback" angle in their reports. One problem players have going into the Super Bowl is the two-week lull between the Conference championships and the grand finale. For over 20 straight weeks—exhibitions, 14 regular-season games and two playoff contests—the Super Bowl finalists play a game a week. Then, in the biggest game of all, they have two weeks to prepare.

That means that the sportswriters and sportscasters who are assigned to cover the Super Bowl have to work hard to dig up stories and try to come up with interesting new angles. Some 1,500 members of the media converged on New Orleans for Super Bowl IX. Many of them arrived a week or so before the game and sought out players for interviews. Naturally quarterbacks are "hot copy," especially Super Bowl newcomers such as Terry.

But it seemed that everyone who interviewed him wanted to use the "dumb quarterback" theme. Nobody was really calling him a dumb quarterback anymore, but they were writing about the fact that this young man who had had to work his way up from No. 3 quarterback on his own team in midseason was now the focal point of the Super Bowl.

"IS BRADSHAW 'TOO DUMB' TO BE SUPER?" demanded a headline in the New York *Times* the week before the game. "MAYBE THIS WILL KILL DUMMY IMAGE—BRADSHAW" read a headline all the way across the page in *The Sporting News* after the Oakland game. And then there was the lady sportscaster who asked Terry point-blank, after he had granted her an exclusive interview, "'Terry, are you really that dumb?" It was her very first question—and her last. Terry just got up from the table and walked away.

It was a shame that a young man who had done so much to turn a whole dormant franchise around should have to face such critics during the most crucial week of his football life. But Terry did.

Coach Chuck Noll did his best to fend off such foolishness.

At one news conference, he stared out to the story-hungry writers and made it clear: "Terry Bradshaw is not dumb. His not being a heady quarterback is a bad rap. It is unfair and unfounded all the way down the line. It hasn't come from anybody in our organization."

But the coach may not have been accurate there, because Pittsburgh reporters, without naming their sources, had quoted Steeler players putting down Terry's ability to run the team. Most of the quotes were from the past, not the hot streak that led the team into the Super Bowl. Nevertheless, the quotes made the newspapers, and Terry and the coach would have to live with them. The more they trickled out, the more Bradshaw had to defend himself.

"If we have a bad game, it's because I'm dumb," he told a New York *Times* sports columnist. "If we have a good game, it's because everybody else played well and I got caught up in the action."

To another writer, he said, "I've had a bellyful of being called a dummy. I hate to talk up for myself, but that's one thing that's really stuck in my craw. They say winning is the true test of a champion and a true test of a great quarterback. . . . The Super Bowl is where everyone evaluates whether you are a winner or a loser, whether you are a good quarterback or a bad one."

And he let that final statement stand for itself as he went out to prepare for the big game. Bradshaw was confident the week before the Super Bowl. He had a good grasp of the game plan to use against the Vikings. And his teammates were finding that his confidence was contagious. The more he believed in himself, the more they believed in him and themselves.

He didn't need to make boastful speeches as Joe Namath did before the 1969 Super Bowl, when the brash New York Jets' quarterback "guaranteed" a victory for his team's followers. Terry wasn't that kind of personality.

"Sure, I could say we are going to crush the Vikings," he said one day. "But let's keep it simple. I don't want to put fire in their eyes."

He went about his business of convincing his own teammates—not the rest of the sports world—of his ability to do the job when it counted most. By game time January 12 he had done just that.

As 80,000 fans poured into Tulane Stadium for the showdown, the winds swirled around the huge oval stadium and the temperature seemed a lot colder than the listed 46 degrees. That was okay with Terry. He wasn't planning to put the ball in the air too much against the Vikings' vicious pass rushers and pesky defensive backs anyway. He was going to run right at that Viking front four, utilizing his powerful backs Harris and Bleier to the utmost.

The Steelers received the opening kickoff, and Terry told himself that right from the start his team could attack the Vikings on the ground. On the first play he sent Harris in to the line for a 5-yard gain and the Steelers were off and running. He tried Harris again on the second down, and Franco might have busted loose for good yardage if he hadn't slipped. Pittsburgh lost the ball after Terry was forced to run out of the pocket by All-Pro end Alan Page, but he had learned that the Vikings could be vulnerable if he stuck to his game plan.

The next time the Steelers got the ball, Terry pitched out to Harris, who was trapped in the backfield for a loss. Bradshaw decided to go for a pass—and selected a screen pass to Frank Lewis, which he completed for an 11-yard gain. He still needed long yardage for the first down, so he dropped back again to throw on third down and was grabbed by the back of the neck by Page. It seemed as if he would be seeing—and feeling —a lot of Page this Sunday afternoon, but Terry didn't seem at all rattled by the experience.

The Steeler defense was doing its best to contain the Vikings, and managed to make life miserable for Tarkenton and his All-Pro running back, Chuck Foreman. In the middle of the first period, the Steeler offense got the ball again, and this time Terry got the team moving. Lewis dropped a hard pass that could have gained some yardage, but Terry came back two plays later with a completion to tight end Larry Brown for a first down. Then, mixing his plays, he got the Steelers within field-goal range, but Roy Gerela's kick was blown off to the left of the goal post.

Undaunted, Terry marched the team into field-goal range again before the quarter was over. Again the three-pointer wasn't converted, because holder Bobby Walden dropped the snap from center.

But the Steelers were moving the ball and that was what counted.

Still, before a national television audience of about 70 million fans, one of the announcers felt it necessary to bring up the "dumb quarterback" theory and explain that Terry wasn't all that bad.

The Steelers' offense moved in the second period, too, though it couldn't score. The Vikings were having worse luck. Tarkenton at one point had completed only three of 12 passes and shortly thereafter fumbled a ball that rolled into the end zone. Tarkenton raced back and pounced on it, but Dwight White promptly pounced on him—for a safety. The Steelers led, 2-0.

Neither team scored for the rest of the first half, but Terry gave the Vikings a sampling of his confidence on the last play of the half. He scrambled for a 17-yard gain, and when he darted into a maze of players from both teams at midfield one wondered if he would come out alive. The ball was dead, the half was over, and just when everyone thought Terry might be dead in the pileup he emerged running for the goal line as the officials whistled desperately for him to stop. He kept right on running, even though the play—and the half—was over.

He had gained more on that play than the whole Viking rushing corps did in the first half. His confidence, along with his faith in the Steelers' defense, bolstered the team during their halftime talk.

Terry and many of the other Steelers changed their shoes before the start of the second half so that they could utilize longer cleats for better footing on the artificial turf that seemed flawed by mushy spots. But that would be the only change that would be made at halftime. The Steelers decided to go right at the Viking defense again. Franco Harris and Rocky Bleier were running well, and Bradshaw was manuevering the team into scoring range, even if the Steelers were having little luck getting on the scoreboard.

A big break came at the start of the second half when the Vikings fumbled the opening kickoff. A Steeler recovered it on the Viking 30-yard line and Terry had his best field position of the day. Bradshaw fed Harris the ball on a slant play into the line, and Franco barreled for 24 yards down to the Viking 6. After a loss, Bradshaw fed Harris again and the 230-pounder rumbled into the end zone for a 9-yard touchdown. The Steeler line was blocking so effectively that Harris went in standing up. The conversion was good and Pittsburgh was suddenly sitting on a 9-0 lead.

For the next 18 minutes, well into the fourth period, the score remained 9-0 as Terry kept feeding the ball to his running backs and they kept eating up time as well as yardage. Terry only threw when necessary and would pass the ball 14 times all day long. But the way he was leading the team—with the help of Harris's outstanding rushing—the Steelers would get about three plays for each two the Vikings got. In a ball-control game, that statistic was important.

The Vikings finally got on the scoreboard with ten and a half minutes to play when one of Bobby Walden's punts was blocked and rolled into the end zone, where it was covered by a Minnesota player. Even though the Steelers were dominating the game, their lead was cut to 9-6. Fortunately, the Vikings failed to make the extra point.

With more than ten minutes to play, and the game still up in the air, Terry Bradshaw took the reins of the team and sealed the victory. He took the team on an 11-play, 66-yard drive. The key plays were his clutch third-down passes—one for 30 yards to tight end Larry Brown and another for 6 to Rocky Bleier. In between, he fed the ball to Harris and Bleier and ate up the clock. With just four and a half minutes remaining in the game, and the drive still in progress, the Steelers were on the Viking 4-yard line with yet another third-down situation.

Terry fired a bullet to Brown in the end zone—and that, for all intents and purposes, was the ball game. Brown grabbed the touchdown pass, Gerela converted, and the Steelers had a 16-6 lead.

The 11-play drive ate up a total of seven minutes. In the waning minutes of the game the Vikings couldn't rally, and that's the way the score stood.

As the jubilant Steelers left the field, the statisticians in the press box began totaling the figures that would tell the story. The Steelers had held the ball for 73 plays compared to only 47 for the Vikings. That helped the Steeler defense in its quest to put a lock on the Vikings' vaunted running attack. As it turned out, the Vikings gained only 21 yards on the ground.

Terry himself had gained 33 yards on five carries. And Harris, the outstanding player in the game according to a press box poll, set Super Bowl records with 34 carries and 158 yards. Rocky Bleier gained 65 more.

The passes Terry had selected so carefully looked good in the statistical columns, too. He connected on nine of 14, mostly at crucial times to keep drives going. And he didn't have an interception to mar his perfect day.

In the locker room later, Terry tried smoking a cigar but kept choking on it as the throngs of well wishers stopped by to congratulate him. Over in another corner of the dressing room, Chuck Noll spoke proudly of his quarterback. "We didn't score a lot of points, but I think Terry did an outstanding job of controlling the ball for us." In essence, the coach was saying that Terry had called a "smart game."

There would be no more stories about dumb quarterbacking. Bradshaw had done his job well.

While most people wanted to talk technical football with him, and he courteously obliged them, Terry had some other comments to make before he closed out his Super Bowl season.

"I've faced a lot of adversity," he said rather seriously to a gathering of reporters. "I withstood the trials and that enabled me, that and my personal faith in God, to do this.

"I've looked at all sides, being a hero and being a jerk. I think I can handle winning the Super Bowl very well."

12 Life with a Winner

If Terry Bradshaw believed in himself as never before after the Super Bowl triumph, his critics wanted to see more before they would admit to his true ability. As a new season dawned the following September, the same old questions lingered on. No more would he have the "dummy image," but national sportswriters still needed to be convinced he had arrived as a standout quarterback with the ability to lead an excellent team throughout an entire season.

Sports Illustrated's writer, in analyzing the National Football League in the magazine's 1975 season preview, mentioned, "Chuck Noll insists that Bradshaw is the official starting quarterback after his performance in the playoffs and the Super Bowl. Sure he is—until he has a bad game or a bad half. . . ."

The Sporting News, in its season preview, was even

tougher on him. "The Steelers lack a comparable offense—and may not have one until Joe Gilliam matures
at quarterback. . . . Terry Bradshaw, their No. 1, is an
interesting case. A remarkable scrambler, Bradshaw
has the ability to throw the ball as straight as Namath
—on a training-camp morning, or, sometimes, if his
primary receiver is wide open. . . . Bradshaw can win
for the Steelers against inferior teams when Pittsburgh's
defense takes complete charge of the game, as it often
does. He is not quite so likely to win against good
teams."

These were harsh criticisms to be leveled at a young
quarterback at the top of his game. But Terry did the
intelligent thing. He decided to answer his critics on
the field, not off it. Words would not be enough.

The Steelers' 1975 schedule was structured in a way
that delayed Terry's hopes to wipe out the criticisms
for a while. The first half of the schedule was loaded
with pushovers—teams such as the San Diego Chargers,
the Cleveland Browns, the Denver Broncos, the Chicago Bears and the Green Bay Packers. San Diego,
Cleveland and Green Bay went through half the 1975
season without winning a game. Chicago was nearly as
bad, and Denver, even with a weak schedule, couldn't
get above .500.

Only the Buffalo Bills, behind O. J. Simpson's great
running and the vast improvement in quarterback Joe
Ferguson, Terry's successor at Woodlawn High School,
had the ability to test the defending Super Bowl champs.
The Bills and the Steelers played in the second game
of the season. The Steelers, coming off a 37-0 opening

day victory over the Chargers, lost to the Bills, 30-21. The rest of the teams could hardly muster up a touchdown against the famed Steel Curtain defense, so Pittsburgh carried a 5-1-0 record into its important November 2 showdown with the Cincinnati Bengals.

The Bengals were undefeated going into the game at their own Riverfront Stadium. Quarterback Ken Anderson, who is younger than Bradshaw, was looking like the best passer in the American Conference. And Cincinnati Coach Paul Brown, the aging genius who taught Noll his football, could be counted on to come up with a game plan that the Steelers would have to respect.

While it wasn't do-or-die for the Steelers, it was test time for Terry and his teammates. Especially Terry. A lot of experts were predicting that the game would be decided by who had the edge at quarterback—Cincinnati with the hot-handed Anderson or Pittsburgh with the vulnerable Bradshaw.

For the first quarter and most of the second 58,000 fans at Riverfront and the critics in the pressbox saw the battle being waged by the defensive units. The score stood 3-3.

For the first time all year Franco Harris was eating up yardage for the Steelers and approaching his first 100-yard game of the season. Cincinnati's offense was centered on Anderson, who was filling the air with passes. As halftime neared, there was no indication that the game would break open. And there was no indication that Bradshaw would play an important role.

But Terry rallied the team in the final seconds. Then, with only eight seconds remaining, Bradshaw sent second-year man Lynn Swann downfield in a desperation attempt. Bradshaw back-pedaled to the 45-yard line of the Bengals and made one of his patented strong-arm throws—just as the sportwriter said he could do on a training-camp morning. Only this one came under game conditions, and Swann, who in 1975 had become Terry's primary receiver, hauled it in and put the finishing touches to a 37-yard touchdown.

Bradshaw connected with Swann again in the third quarter, this time for 25 yards and a touchdown. The Steelers pushed ahead, 17-3. After that, Terry was content to stay on the ground for the most part, utilizing Harris's refound strength and the solid running of Rocky Bleier. The team marched downfield again in the third period with Bleier scoring.

When Cincinnati came back to bring the score to 23-17, Bradshaw went to work again and marched the team into range of the end zone. He carried the last yard for a touchdown himself. The Steelers won the game, 30-24.

Much to his surprise, Terry was complimented by one of the sportswriters afterward for calling such a good game. "An intelligent game" were the words used. Bradshaw accepted the words and smiled. He had finally made a believer.

In the next three weeks Bradshaw would have a chance to put the critics to rest for good. His Steelers would face the surprising Houston Oilers, who had become the most improved team in football, the Kansas

City Chiefs and the Oilers again. There would be no letup in pressure on him.

Terry responded to the test as he never had before. He took complete control in all three games. In the first match against Houston, he threw three touchdown passes in a 24-17 triumph. The last of the scoring throws was to John Stallworth, with only 38 seconds left in the game. Against the Chiefs, who had come on strong after a mediocre start, Terry drove the Steelers 86 yards in the waning minutes of the first half and capped the drive with a 42-yard pass to Swann with a mere seven seconds left on the clock. Then, against the Oilers again on a Monday night nationally televised game, Terry guided his team to a 32-9 manhandling of the upstart Oilers.

It was Pittsburgh's eighth straight win—all of them with Bradshaw at the controls. The final victory in that skein, against the Oilers, had the critics rethinking. Bradshaw had connected on 13 of 16 passes.

Statistics don't win games, but sometimes they help win over critics. The game's figures brought Terry's season to over 2 percent completions, the best in football. His interception rate for the year was a minuscule 3.4 percent of his passes attempted, also one of the best marks in the league. He was guiding a great team to a great year, another plus for him. And to show how well everyone knew it he was named Steelers' Player of the Year.

He could say confidently and proudly, "I feel very much at home out there. I never felt like that before."

How much he felt at home on the field was decisive in Pittsburgh winding up with another championship season. The Steelers qualified for Super Bowl X by eliminating the Oakland Raiders, and then faced the Dallas Cowboys sparked by the redoubtable Roger Staubach. Though the Steelers beat Oakland, they suffered a serious loss in the game when Swann suffered a concussion.

For two weeks after the game, Swann said, "I couldn't get loose, I had no concentration." Bradshaw, agreeing, added, "He couldn't even catch a cold."

But on January 18, 1976, before 80,000 fans in the Miami Orange Bowl and a TV audience estimated at 75-million, both Swann and Bradshaw truly cut loose against dazzling sets of formations and plays by the Cowboys. The Steelers' defense was as strong as it had been all season, but early in the last quarter the Cowboys were ahead 10-7.

Then Pittsburgh rallied. A safety and a field goal inched the Steelers ahead, 12-10—no safe margin in light of the Cowboys' skilled game.

The most spectacular play came in the final quarter when Bradshaw passed 59 yards for a leaping touchdown catch by Swann. The defense flattened Bradshaw on the throw, so dazing him that he did not know if Swann had caught the ball. The next he knew he was in the locker room, out of the game for its few remaining minutes. And the next he knew after that the locker room was filled with jubilant Steelers celebrating their 21-17 win over Dallas and their second Super Bowl victory.

Index

Aillet, Joe, 25–26
Anderson, Ken, 101, 123

Badish, Melissa, 70
Bleier, Rocky, 57, 98, 106, 108,
    115, 118, 119, 124
Blount, Mel, 47, 57
Bradshaw, Bill, 7, 8–9, 13–14, 15,
    17, 20, 109
Bradshaw, Craig, 13
Bradshaw, Gary, 13–14
Bradshaw, Novice, 15, 16
Bradshaw, Terry
  birth, 14
  childhood, 13–15
  early sports, 12–13, 14–17
  high school football, 16–22
  college football, 22–35
  college all-star games, 36–37, 39,
    60–61
  scouted by pros, 32, 33, 34, 36–
    37, 38–40, 41–45, 48
  and Pittsburgh Steelers, 7–11,
    72–78, 79–90, 91–96, 96–110,
    115–20, 122–25
  drafted, 50, 53–56, 57–58
  contract negotiation, 46–47,
    55–56
  rookie year, 59–69, 73

personal characteristics, 9–11,
    54–55, 113–14, 115, 121
statistics, 21, 31, 35, 68, 78, 119,
    125
Brandt, Gil, 39–40
Brown, Larry, 71, 103, 116, 119
Brown, Paul, 56, 77, 123
Buffalo Bills, 105–7

Chomyszak, Steve, 94
Cockroft, Don, 84

Dallas Cowboys, 126
Davis, O.K. (Buddy), 24, 35
Dudley, Bill, 42

Edwards, Glen, 71

Fears, Tom, 32
Foreman, Chuck, 116
Fuqua, John (Frenchy), 57, 75,
    78, 82, 83, 84, 86, 88

Gabriel, Roman, 45
Gerela, Roy, 71, 85, 87, 106, 116,
    119
Gilliam, Joe, 93, 95, 96–98, 100,
    102, 104, 107, 108, 122
Greene, Joe, 41, 71, 83, 94, 102,
    104-5
Griese, Bob, 61, 77, 91–92

Ham, Jack, 71, 83
Hanratty, Terry, 44, 48, 54–55, 62,
    66, 67–68, 75, 76, 77, 80, 90,
    93, 94, 95, 97, 101–2, 102–3
Harris, Franco, 82, 83, 84, 85, 86,
    88, 98, 103, 106, 108, 115,
    116, 118, 119, 123, 124
Hedges, Lee, 16, 17–18, 20
Hughes, Dennis, 74

Jones, Bert, 24–25
Jones, Dub, 24, 25, 31

Kemp, Jackie, 53
Klosterman, Don, 39, 40

Lambright, Max, 26, 27, 34
Layne, Bobby, 51, 52–53
Leahy, Bob, 75, 77–78
Lewis, Frank, 71, 81, 82, 83, 84,
    101, 103, 116
Louisiana Tech Bulldogs, 22, 23–
    24, 26, 27-31, 33–35

McMakin, John, 86
Mansfield, Ray, 64, 107–8, 111
Miami Dolphins, 89–90
Minnesota Vikings, 111, 112, 115–
    20
Mullins, Gerry, 71, 89

Namath, Joe, 34, 40, 53–54, 61,
    67, 72, 73, 80–81, 111
National Football League (NFL)
    8, 36, 38–45, 47–48, 96, 101,
    104
  playoffs
    (1972), 87–90
    (1974), 105–9
Nix, Kent, 48, 55, 62
Noll, Chuck, 8, 39, 40, 52, 56–58,
    60–61, 66, 70, 72, 75, 76,
    79–80, 92, 98, 99, 101, 102,
    103, 107, 113–14, 120, 121,
    123

Oakland Raiders, 87–89, 107, 108–
    9, 126

Parilli, Vito (Babe), 71–74, 75, 96
Pearson, Preston, 57, 82, 111
Pittsburgh Steelers, 7–9, 10, 11, 37,
    39, 41–42, 44–45, 47, 50–53
    1969 season, 40–41, 51–52
    1970 season, 57, 62–68
    1971 season, 70ff., 75–78
    1972 season, 79–90
    1973 season, 93–96
    1974 season, 96–109, 115–20
    1975 season, 122–25
Pugh, Robert, 7, 46, 55

Robertson, Phil, 25, 26, 27
Rooney, Art, Sr., 44, 47, 50, 52, 70
Rooney, Dan, 7, 8, 9, 41, 45, 48
    56, 70
Rozelle, Pete, 44–45

Senior Bowl All-Star Game
    (1970), 36–37, 39, 40
Shanklin, Ron, 47, 57, 64, 66, 77,
    78, 80, 82, 86, 101
Shiner, Dick, 48, 55, 57
Shula, Don, 62, 63
Simpson, O.J., 105, 106, 122
Slaughter, Mickey, 27, 62, 72
Spinks, Tommy, 17, 18–19, 20–21,
    22, 23, 24, 25, 26–27, 28
Stabler, Ken, 87–88
Staggers, Jon, 47, 57
Staubach, Roger, 126
Super Bowl, 8, 9, 110–13, 114
    IX (1975), 9, 10, 115-20
    X (1976), 126
Swann, Lynn, 106, 108, 124, 125,
    126

Tarkenton, Fran, 31, 111, 117
Thomas, J. T., 02

Unitas, Johnny, 53

Van Brocklin, Norm, 41

Wagner, Mike, 71
Walden Bobby, 116, 118

Young, Al, 90

Date Due

STS=MAR 88				
8/20/99				

Cat. No. 23 231   Printed in U.S.A.